The
Great
Tribulation

By
Chike Udolisa

Copyright © 2013 by Chike Udolisa

The Great Tribulation
by Chike Udolisa

Printed in the United States of America

ISBN 9781628391121

All rights reserved solely by the author. The author guarantees all contents are original and do not infringe upon the legal rights of any other person or work. No part of this book may be reproduced in any form without the permission of the author. The views expressed in this book are not necessarily those of the publisher.

All Scriptures are from the King James Version (KJV) of the Bible except where otherwise indicated. Other versions referred to are:

AV–Amplified Version
Copyright © 1954, 1958, 1962, 1964, 1965, 1987 by The Lockman Foundation
NIV–New International Version. Used by permission. All rights reserved.
New International Version (NIV). Copyright © 1973, 1978, 1984, 2011 by Biblica, Inc.™ . Used by permission. All rights reserved.
NASV- New American Standard Version
Copyright © 1960, 1962, 1963, 1968, 1971, 1972, 1973, 1975, 1977, 1995 by The Lockman Foundation. Used by permission. All rights reserved.

www.xulonpress.com

8 CHIKE UDOLISA 1998

Anyone who feels impressed of the LORD to contribute immensely in the production and/or distribution of this book for the sake of the saints on this side of eternity, may please contact the author via the following e-mail

chikeudolisa@gmail.com;
Tracker12tracker@yahoo.co.uk

Contents

SECTION A – KEY FACTS ON THE GREAT TRIBULATION . . . ix
    Preface ix
1.0   Introduction 11
2.0   Understanding Daniel's Seventy Weeks Prediction 18
3.0   The Timing and Important Features of the Great Tribulation . . . 26
3.1   Jesus's Account of the Tribulation from the Gospels 28
3.1.1 Descriptive Impression of Jesus Account 29
3.1.2 Facts Supporting Jesus Account 30
3.2   John's Account of the Tribulation as Recorded in the
       Book of Revelations 31
3.2.1 The Presumed Rapture of the Church before the Tribulation . . . 33
3.2.2 Facts Supporting John's Account 34

SECTION B – KEY PLAYERS IN THE GREAT TRIBULATION . . 37
4.0   The Contention of the Two Great
       Cities in the Great Sea (*the Waters*) 37
5.0   Enter…the Dragon (Rev. 13) 43
5.1.1 John's Account 43
5.1.2 Daniel's Account 44
5.1.3 Correlation of John's and Daniel's Accounts 45
5.2   The Seven–Headed Beast 46
5.3   The False Prophet of the Seven–Headed Beast 48
6.0   Introducing the Great Whore (Mystery Babylon) 54
6.1   The Nature the Whore's Activities 57
6.2   The Whore as the Mother, Initiator, Source or
       Brain Behind All the Abominations on Earth 57
6.3   The Whore as the Mother, Initiator, Source and
       '*Sustainer*' of the World System and Commerce 59

SECTION C – APPLICATION		**69**
7.0	The Nature of the Great Tribulation	69
7.1	Contemporary Application and Impact on the Church	69
7.2	The Essence of Our Being	76
7.3	The Pathway to Follow (Put on your Wedding Garment)	78
A.	Where a Man's Heart is	78
B.	Where a Man's Eye is – Our Focus	80
C.	Loving Either God or Mammon	80
D.	Seeking After the Things of this Life or After the Kingdom of God [Your Pursuits in Life]	82
E.	The Process	83
F.	The Place of the Holy Spirit	85
8.0	CONCLUSION	89

TO

GOD

BE THE GLORY

TO

THE CHURCH

AND TO

MY WIFE AND EVERY ONE THAT

CONTRIBUTED IN NO LITTLE MEASURE TO

THIS WORK

BE EVERLASTING BLESSING

Section A

Key Facts on the Great Tribulation

—⚏—

PREFACE

Sometime ago, in the course of God's revelation of the things that are written in this book, I was privileged in a vision to be invited to heaven for the marriage feast of the Son of God. I cannot explain how I was transported into that realm but I suddenly saw myself before the being that appeared to be the Lord of host, surrounded by the members of His family, all dressed in white. The being asked me "Where is your wedding garment?" It dawned on me that I was apparently not dressed in white. He repeated the question again and I could not answer. At the end of the third repetition, I said inside my heart, "I do not have my wedding garment on, do unto me that which is just and right." Immediately after this, He opened His mouth to pronounce a just judgment, but the Son of God to whose feast we were gathered intervened and said, "Father, please give him one more opportunity to go back and put on his wedding garment." The Lord of host then agreed and said to me, ***"Go back and put on your wedding garment and tell your brethren to do likewise."*** I was then led down back to earth.

When I came back to myself I was visibly shaken and afraid for myself and all my brethren. Before this time the Holy Spirit had been taking me line-by-line, precept-upon-precept through all the statements of Jesus in the red-letter edition of the gospel of Mathew, interpreting each beyond what I had ever known of them in the nine years of my receiving Jesus as personal Lord and Savior at that time. At about the same time, I had presented a quest and yearning to the Holy Spirit "that I wanted to see the world and more particularly, the situation in the churches, from His own perspective." As I progressed in studying the scriptures, I came by Mathew 20:16 where He said that "many are called but few are chosen." Then I was afraid of what I would be taught by the Holy Spirit if I asked Him for expatiation, so I skipped it, only to meet it again in Mathew 22:14. At this point, I could not escape the conviction to ask for further explanation. By the time the Holy Spirit started on this, I was so afraid of the things I heard. It was in the course of this divine explanation that I received the insight into the **Great Tribulation** recorded in this book. I was so shocked to recognize that after nine years of being born again and sincerely following after a host of the things we had been taught in Christendom, I was yet to be clothed with the wedding garments that I needed to meet with Christ.

This led to further agonizing and yearning to understand the negating factors before me and the church, and to possibly see the struggles of the church in the current world system from *God's perspective*. The events of the ensuing revelations and teachings by the Holy Spirit covered many months and years. Over and over again, I pleaded with the Holy Spirit to confirm what He was teaching me, for some of these were at variance with some of the things we had been taught in Christendom for many years. I made it clear to Him that I would not want to imbibe or be a party to the spread of a false doctrine. In response, He started taking me from one part of the scriptures to another to confirm all He was teaching me. He also brought my way, Watchman Nee's book on *"Love Not the World"*, which confirmed the fabric of what He was teaching me. For over twenty years, He has continued to confirm them from different parts of the scriptures up to this very time of it being recorded in this entire book.

It is my earnest prayer that as we go through the records of this book, the Holy Spirit will open the eyes of our understanding that we may see where we stand from God's perspective. For many of us may have fallen short of the promise to enter into His rest without knowing it. This book will therefore help us to see clearly into God's perspective of the state of the church as a body and as individuals in our present world. Should you prefer not to open up for God to help you examine your life before the silver cord be broken, please do not bother to read this book.

Chapter One

1.0 Introduction

—⚝—

At the tail end of Christ's ministry on earth, He began to prepare the disciples for His departure and His second coming. He assured them that He is going to come back to take them that believed in Him[1]. To drive home this point beyond all reasonable doubts, He promised to send down to them the Holy Spirit as a seal guaranteeing an inheritance with Him in God[2]. This blessed hope we all know and believe to be undisputable according to the immutability of God's counsel[3]. Having assured them of the provision of eternal habitations for them, *he did not stop short of calling their attention* **TO ALL THE RESISTANCE** *they would face in their life time,* in their bid to obtain this promised eternal habitation.

From accounts scattered in various parts of the gospels, He made it clear to them that they will face the resistance of false teachers and false prophets in the church[4]. These He remarked, will succeed in turning the hearts of many away from the sound truth, thereby making them lose their eternal habitation.

Describing the signs of the end of times, He made it clear that iniquity will abound; *as a result, many believers shall fall away, departing from the truth, giving heed to seducing spirits and doctrines of demons.* Further in the scriptures it is written, men shall become more deceitful than ever before, unholy, covetous, high minded and lovers of themselves and of pleasure more than lovers of God. False teachers, prophets (and ministers) will abound among the believers who will, as a result of their covetousness, deceitfully make merchandise of the brethren. The picture painted here is that there will be so much wickedness and iniquity and gross darkness shall overtake all of mankind to turn the hearts of all men (*including the believers*) away from the truth of God and the promise of His eternal habitation[5].

If therefore deceit will abound and false prophets and teachers will teach and practice deceit under the cloak of Christ as though it is the Spirit of Chirst that is teaching and prophesying, then we face a very imminent danger of high casualty in our Christian warfare. The reason is simple: it is easier to fight an enemy you know than it is to fight the enemy you don't **recognize**. Many mighty warriors that have fought and won many battles have fallen at the feet of the enemy they didn't recognize as enemies. Such examples are seen in Samson's life[6] and Eglon, king of Moab[7]. As Christ foretold, many false teachings and doctrines of demons have infiltrated into the rank and file of the churches. These have been unfortunately taught and encouraged by some highly respected ministers and are well received among us as sound (scriptural). Meanwhile, these false teachings and prophesies have eaten into the fabrics of the churches and is resulting in our present decay, schisms, fascisms, worldliness and *'merchandization'* of the gospel of Christ. Yet we all seem so careless and at ease with all these facts. This is the same kind of decay and rottenness God discovered in the Israelites when He said concerning them that "the prophets prophesy falsely, and the priests (pastors) rule on their own authority, and my people love it so..."[8]. As a matter of fact, the same decay and rottenness that rocked the Israelites under the old covenant has taken hold of the churches in these end times, this notwithstanding the fact that we are operating under a better covenant.

Unknown to us, as Christ predicted, the enemy has planted himself within the church and it has become hard for us to recognize the spirit of the enemy in operation. With this strategy, our enemy has so succeeded in deceiving and confusing us from within and from without, about the warfare we are engaged in, as Christians. ***In the scriptures, this great resistance against God's place in the lives of the saints and against all godliness is what is referred to as the Great Tribulation***. This warfare is what we refer to in this book as the ***Great Tribulation*** *and the scriptural facts to buttress this view are presented in this book.*

Today however, and among us in Christendom, there has been much misconception and conflicting ideologies on the issues concerning this Great Tribulation. It is not surprising to see so much deception and diverse doctrines abounding among the believers as Jesus had earlier made clear that such will abound in the end times. And the enemy's target is to stop us from making it to the eternal habitation which Christ promised us. When Jesus was asked about the signs of the end times, He kept stressing the prevalence of this ***deception*** rooted along with the ***mystery of iniquity***, which will cause many to derail from the truth. As a result, we were later instructed in the scriptures to give all diligence to make our calling and election sure; so that we may be among the few chosen ones from the many that were called. For even as it is written; ***the righteous shall scarcely be saved*** [9].

The essence of this book is for us to understand particularly *the subtle activities* of our enemy–the prince of this world–with respect to this great resistance (or great tribulation). He has succeeded in blind-folding so many of us from the truth about it. As a result, he is destroying many in the churches today as an undiagnosed virus.

The church today has embraced more than six different views about the proceedings of the great tribulation and details of how it will play out. While making each school of thought to be backed by reasonable assertions, our enemy has succeeded in making the church relegate to the background, important facts concerning the great tribulation; presenting them as issues of the future that will not necessarily in any way affect our salvation. ***This is deceit at work!*** The devil seems to have succeeded in making the church believe that:

1. The events of the great tribulation will most likely take place after we have left earth and/or

2. The church will partake in the great tribulation, but that this event is still in the future.

However, going through the scriptures we discovered that the great tribulation has already started! It is an on-going event which the saints have been going through and will continue to go through until the rapture. This distortion of the truth and confusion brought in by our enemy upon the churches has made us cast **RESTRAINT** to the winds, since we feel it does not concern us. Therefore, we have become like people that are infected with the AIDS virus and are yet ignorantly expecting the virus to come into existence in the future. Slowly, however many of us are dying daily because of this virus. ***This measure of deception is so prevalent in Christendom and would continue till the rapture.***

A major point of concern is that the saints seem not to be fully aware of the things that constitute the great tribulation and the nature of this event. ***My prayer is that we will come to the knowledge of the fact that the substantive core of the "Great Tribulation" which we are expecting to come in the future consists of the entire operation of "Deception and Mystery Iniquity" which is already at work.*** Both of them are inseparable because the latter is the strategy for executing the agenda of the former. The presence of one indicates the presence of the other.

As a result of this present great tribulation, many of us are today drunk with the wine of 'mystery Babylon' (the whole corrupt system of this world–***mystery iniquity***). Yet we are un-aware of this fact. This is the cause of the present corruption, immorality, lasciviousness, deceit, rancor, pursuit of pleasure and materialism among us today in the churches. Our delight, yearnings and cravings are more after the things of this world than after Christ (or heavenly things). We yearn to be rich, claim to be rich and increased with goods, and have need of nothing. In-fact being rich has become our measure for godliness. Yet we do not know that we are wretched, miserable, poor, blind, and naked. For most of us, our focus is on the things we possess–food, clothing, shelter, fame, career, etc. Constrained by this World System, we have paid so much attention to miracles, healings and prosperity for solutions to our pressures, though their contribution is merely to the flesh. I hope you are beginning to see the strategy of the enemy at work; because these are part of the things that make up the great tribulation. This was what informed the declaration by Jesus: that if we make friends with the ungodly mammon, when we die, they will receive us in their eternal habitations[10]. The great battle is raging and the saints need to wake up to this reality.

I am persuaded that after going through the record of this book we will all have cause as a church to cry out unto the Lord our God, day and night saying, "Forgive our failures and avenge us of our disgrace, decay and desecration." Will the Lord not hear us? He will, and that quickly! But I have heard a cry in the heavens saying: "to whom is the arm of the Lord made known, who has believed our message and whom shall I send?"

The understanding recorded here over the years concerning the great tribulation is not because of any righteousness of my own or hard work but simply the working of God's grace and mercy towards us all to the intent that the body of Christ may know and understand God's perspective on this subject. As for me, I am an unprofitable servant and have only done that which I was instructed to do. May the Lord grant us understanding as we proceed.

Meanwhile, ponder over these declarations which came forth in the process of the things the Lord taught me regarding the great tribulation:

> *The earnest intention and expectation of the LORD regarding us all is that we will all be a perfect replication of His being; that our whole being would be consumed and engrossed with this singular pursuit after Him. Nothing else is worth living for. Every other purpose in life is but emptiness, vanity, worthless, and meaningless. They are but a pursuance*

after shadow; a striving after the wind. Behold all the innumerable, immeasurable, unfathomable, and boundless godly virtues that our Father has made available for us in Christ. This notwithstanding, we are so weak, frail, ineffective, and of a truth poor, miserable, and unproductive. Therefore, we should cry and bemoan our state; for the mystery of iniquity presently at work, has wrecked and devastated us.

If only we had quietly waited before His THRONE without much distraction, then would we have been steadily led into the depths of His being. For all the secret things and mysteries of the kingdom of heaven, and the FORM of the most High, are His free gift to us in Christ Jesus. Yet no one seems so eager to pursue and to lay hold on these excellent treasures. This is because the mystery of iniquity would not want to allow any of us to accomplish this feat. Thus, the ensuing decay of godliness in the churches today, is an indication that the grand deceptive movement of the devil has been effective to the extent of deceiving, confusing, and swallowing up many.

The essence of this book is to help prepare the saints for the second coming of Christ or to meet the Lord (which so ever comes first). The time to wake up from our slumber, stupor and indolence is now!

Therefore I am in agony for myself and my beloved brethren. I beat my heart as I remember this decay among the sons and daughters of Zion. Why have we forgotten that he who warreth does not entangle himself with the affairs of everyday life? Ah, God, when will you turn our captivity again? But how are the mighty fallen in the midst of the battle, and the weapons of our warfare perish. This has been told in hell, and in the streets of Babylon, so did the daughters of hell rejoice and the angels of darkness exult. Oh ye sons of righteousness weep over the decay and desolation of Zion. Ye mountains of Zion, let there be no dew or rain upon you; for from you the sons and daughters of Zion derailed and would not turn back. The cankerworm, the locust, the caterpillar, and the palmer worm have gone through the land and we have become rotten and saltless. Our strength from the Lord is vanished and the glory of His presence is departed from His mountain.

If I should forget thee, O beloved brethren of Zion, then let my whole being forget her vocation. If I would not remember thee then let me lose my speech that I may wait before our Father and be silent, peradventure

> *I may obtain mercy for our salvation and the balm of Gilead for our healing. Oh Jehovah, thou whose name alone art JEHOVAH, arise I plead; avenge our course against our enemy, for she has glorified herself over your place in us. Behold she has crushed, swallowed, and made empty vessels your 'delicates'–the very children of your labour.*

Brethren, this should be our hearts' cry. For this reason Jesus asked: when the Son of Man shall come, shall He find such ones on earth?[11] I pray He finds you and me in this category and not in the category of them that shall be engrossed and overcharged with the cares and necessities of the things of this life. For such are they that shall be caught drunk with the wine of Mystery Babylon – *the grand effect of the great tribulations of our time.*

In the successive pages, our focus will be on outlining according to a biblical context, the view of God in these issues, making occasional references to other Christian views on these issues, to diffuse all our differences. Aware of how controversial this subject matter is, we would start our discussion with Daniel's seventy–week predictions on Israel knowing that most divergent views on the timing and details of the great tribulation find their roots in this prophecy. However, recognizing that it is too intellectual and could derail the flow of this book, we will concentrate only on issues relevant to the timing of the events therein. We will then proceed to consider the accounts of Jesus and John on the timing of the great tribulation as recorded in the Gospels and Revelation respectively and correlating the accounts of John with that of Daniel. For further clarification on the subject matter, we will also undertake an extensive exposition of the woman and dragon of Revelation 12, the beast and false prophet of Revelation 13 and the 'whore' (mystery Babylon) of Revelation 17. Thereafter, we will zero in on understanding the nature of the great tribulation and the overwhelming presence and influence of the whore in this present great tribulation upon the churches; showing clearly, how many of us may have been overtaken by our enemy, and are identified with the mark of the beast, even without our knowing it. Finally, by God's grace, we will look at the pathway God will have us tread, in these present times, if we must escape all these dangers that have come upon our generation and be able to stand before Christ at His coming without guile, spot, wrinkle, or any blemish.

I pray that God will give us listening ears and an understanding mind as we go through this study; that we may all be able to grasp the intricacies of the dangers facing us and be able to wash our robes clean and white, that nothing may beset us from the hope that is set before us.

END NOTES

1. Jn.14:1-3;
2. Jn.14:26; 16:7,13; Eph.1:13-14.
3. Heb.6:17
4. Matt.24:11, Mark 13:21-23, Luke 21:8
5. Acts 20:29-30; 1 Tim.4:1-2, 2 Tim.3:1-9, 2 Pet.2:13;
6. Judg.16
7. Judg.3:12-30
8. Jer.5:31 NASV
9. 1 Pet.4:18
10. Lk.16:9
11. Lk.18:8

Chapter Two

2.0 Understanding Daniel's Seventy Weeks Prediction

Daniels seventy week prediction as recorded in the ninth chapter of the book of Daniel has over time been the basis of most divergent views on the great tribulation held in Christendom today. Some of these include:

1. The thought that we are yet to see the beginning of the last week of Daniel's seventy-week prophecy i.e that time was suspended to enable grace abound from the moment the Messiah was cut off and will only resume after the rapture. Here it is presumed that it is after the church has been raptured that the great tribulation will commence and last for seven years.

2. Another thought is that since the Messiah was cut off, we have been in the first-half of the last week of Daniel's seventy-week prophecy. Here it is believed that the next event being expected is the secret rapture of the saints. This rapture is believed to mark the end of the first-half of the last week of Daniel's seventy-week prophecy. The fulfilment of this event is also expected to mark the beginning of the great tribulation which is then expected to continue for the second-half of the last week of Daniel's seventy-week prophecy

Most interpretations put the events of the great tribulation in the future and it is believed that this seventy-week prophecy will stop at the end of the world.

2.0 Understanding Daniel's Seventy Weeks Prediction

It has become necessary to clearly understand these predictions in the book of Daniel and to put them in their clear perspective. The records of Daniel 9 show that Daniel was studying the prophetic scripts of Jeremiah chapters 25–33. His attention was drawn particularly to the fact *that it had been appointed unto Isreal to stay in the captivity that started from King Nebuchadnezzar's time for seventy years[1] and that after this period, God would cause Isreal and Judah to return to the land He gave to their fathers[2]. The Lord went on further to explain the troubles the people of Judah and Isreal would go through in this captivity, indeed He called it "the time of Jacob's trouble"[3]*. These scriptures simply state that after the appointed seventy years, He will visit them, to return them to the land of His promise. Then they will call upon Him and He will answer them, they will seek Him and find Him[4]. In that day, He shall restore them, make a new covenant with them[5], make an end of their sin[6], establish His righteousness in their hearts[7] and establish Isreal again as a holy place unto Him[8]. This in a nutshell, is what Daniel understood from the book of Jeremiah. He also realized and acknowledged that this seventy years desolation of Isreal had indeed been grievous. But it was more painful for Daniel to discover that no one seem concerned at that time about Jacob's trouble, as to plead their case that they may be healed at the end of the seventy years[9].

This was what constrained Daniel to cry out unto God for mercy for his people, the Isrealites, with all manner of prayer and suplications and with fasting, sackcloth and ashes. In this prayer he acknowledged the grievousness of this desolation (Jacob's trouble[10]). He also acknowledged all the iniquities his people had committed against God[11] and the defilement of the holy city of their God[12].

Thereafter he started appealing unto God for mercy, forgiveness, and healing while summarizing the essence of his prayer, fasting and suplications, making it clear that:

1. He is confessing the sin of his people, ISREAL and

2. making supplication for the restoration and reconsecration of the holy mountain of his God (i.e thy City or Jerusalem[13]). In Ezekiel this sanctuary was clearly called the most holy place[14].

After Daniel set himself unto much prayer with fasting concerning this prophecy of Jeremiah, angel Gabriel was sent to make him understand

Jeremiah's prophecy which provides answers to the second aspect of his prayer i.e restoration of Israel. Then angel Gabriel stated:

> *Seventy weeks are determined upon thy people and upon thy holy city, to finish the transgression, and to make an end of sins, and to make reconciliation for iniquity, and to bring in everlasting righteousness, and to seal up the vision and prophecy, and to anoint the most Holy.*[15]

This verse made it clear that for His people the Israelites and their holy city Jerusalem the following actions have been determined:

1. to finish their transgressions

2. to make an end of their sins

3. to make reconciliation for their iniquity

4. to bring in everlasting righteousness among his people

5. to seal (finish, fulfil, accomplish) the vision and prophesy

6. to anoint(rededicate) the most holy(or holy mountain of his God-vs.16)

Here, Gabriel provided graphical explanations to Daniel on the prophesy and vision that was given by Jeremiah concerning the people of Israel, making it clear that it will completely be fulfilled (accomplished) by the end of the seventy weeks appointed. This script of note has unfortunately been misconceived as referring to a time frame in the relationship between God and all mankind that will culminate at the end of the world, rather than a time frame in the relationship between God and the Israeli nation as clearly specified by Jeremiah. Therefore, the seventy weeks has been interpreted by many to mean that once started, will be completed at the end of the world, but this is not the picture painted here by Gabriel. The subject matter in this verse is, **"*thy people*" (*Israel*) and "*thy holy city*"(*Jerusalem*) and the making of an end to the sin of the Israelites by the sacrifice of the Messiah**. All that is written therein actually concerns Israel and not the whole world and also not the end of all prophecy in the world, but the end of the prophecy of Jeremiah, which Daniel had been considering, (this was what Gabriel came to explain to him). The essence of these clarifications is to lay the foundation that will help us correct the notion that, the timing of the Great Tribulation is in the future.

2.0 Understanding Daniel's Seventy Weeks Prediction

EVENTS OF THE SEVENTY WEEKS

In the record of prophecy and history, commandment was first given by Cyrus to restore the whole city of Jerusalem: the streets, the knocked down houses, temple and walls; to restore life normally again in Jerusalem before the coming of the Messiah. This order to rebuild Jerusalem marked the beginning of the seventy-week prediction in Daniel (broken down in seven weeks, sixty-two weeks, and one week). As indicated, the Messiah was to be cut off after the seven and sixty-two weeks; the people of the prince that was to come would destroy Jerusalem again in the remaining week. Within that week, the prince would observe the covenant with the people of Israel and in the midst of it, break it and cause the people to cease from observing the covenant. By this act and the destruction of the city and sanctuary, the people become desolate. *This marked the end of the seventy weeks* (i.e the end of the remaining one week). Then he made it clear that this desolation will remain in force till the end of the world when the vengeance detailed by God shall be meted on the *desolator* and the desolate[16].

In the verses cited above, Gabriel was giving explanations to Daniel (and now to us as Jesus said"...whoso readeth, let him understand"[17]) concerning the plan of God prophesied long ago through Jeremiah in respect of the Israelites' continued stubbornness. The Lord wants us to understand that His people have continued to sin and break His covenant, like their fathers. After so much warning through their prophets including Isaiah and Jeremiah, they remained stiff necked, their hearts were bent on turning away and their continual sacrifices were not able to make any change in their hearts. Thus God, decided that He will banish them from the land so that the land may rest from the iniquities of His people for seventy years[18]. God however made it clear that He had another plan of restoration for this people. After seventy years in captivity He planned and appointed a "seventy-week" period within which they would go back to their land and make preparations for another covenant that will make a perfect end to their continual sinning and transform them to live righteously before Him forever. This covenant was to be sealed in the blood of the lamb of God (the Messiah), that taketh away the sins of the world. This was why the Messiah had to come to make atonement for their sins (past and present); to make an end of their sinning; to reconcile them unto His Father; and to bring into them a righteouness that will last forever. The author of the book of Hebrews confirmed this[19].This very picture is the same that was painted by the vision of Jeremiah from chapters 25-33. This prophecy does not however negate the fact that there were other prophecies in the scriptures indicating that the coming of the Messiah to put an end to sin, was not only meant for the Isrealites, but also for whosoever would believe from the whole gentile world. The very prophecy under consideration here however, refers solely to the Isrealites and to the things that will happen to them after the Messiah is caught up.

Unfortunately, in accordance with the prophecy given by angel Gabriel, the children of Israel rejected the Messiah and turned down this covenant the Lord designed to make with them. This notwithstanding, the Messiah established the new covenant for which He came, sealed it in His blood and opened the door to the gentiles to benefit from this covenant. Therefore, the kingdom of God (which also means *making an end of sin, reconciliation unto God, and instilling of everlasting righteousness*) was taken from Israel and given to other nations that would bring forth the desired fruits[20]. Jesus confirmed in Matthew[21] what angel Gabriel explained to Daniel; that Jerusalem shall remain desolate till the end of age when Christ will come again triumphantly. He further makes it clear that because they turned down this new covenant which the Messiah came to establish with them, God will turn towards all the high streets (i.e all other nations of the earth) and they who were "not my people" will become "my people", while the people for whom the covenant was initially made for become cast away[22].

A school of thought believes that "the making of an end to sin, reconciliation unto God, instilling of everlasting righteousness and anointing of the most holy place" is still in the future when Christ will come for the millennial reign, and therefore extrapolated the remaining week of the "seventy-week" period to a time in the future. If we accept this point of view, it will negate the tenets of the covenant the Messiah came to enact. To every covenant there are not less than two parties involved. Each party has a contribution to make for the fulfilment of the covenant. This covenant in question was designed to put an end to sin in the life of every man who accepts the covenant; and to establish everlasting righteousness in them–for the Jews first and for the Gentiles[23]. The first covenant sealed by the blood of bulls and goats could not bring about the desired end to sin. But this new covenant, sealed in the blood of the Messiah is effective through the Holy Spirit to put an end to sin[24]. Thus the offering of the Messiah and the provision of the Holy Spirit was God's part to the covenant to ensure that the yoke of sin over man is broken and that an ever-lasting righteousness is enthroned in their hearts through the reign of His Spirit. The person who enters into this covenant has to believe and abide (i.e remain) in Him[25] as this is a requirement to ensure the efficacy of the covenant.

It takes the contribution of both parties, to fulfil the covenant. If therefore today we are not living holy, (i.e an end to sin in our lives is not seen, neither do we walk in everlasting righteousness, or the most holy tabernacle of God in us is not consecrated), it is not because a holy designated covenant (with all its instruments) capable of putting an 'end to sin' and to instil everlasting righteousness has not been instituted, or that God has not fulfilled His part in making us His holy habitation, but that we have not kept to our own part of the covenant. Should we lower the standard and purpose of the new covenant simply for the reason of our inadequacies? God forbid! The covenant is holy and it is designed to make holy all the parties to the covenant. An account in John indicates clearly that whosoever committeth sin is a servant of the devil[26]. But that He, the Messiah, came to put an end to sin and to establish the supremacy of an ever-lasting righteousness upon them that will believe and keep step with the Spirit of the covenant which He came to enact. God has established and provided all that is required for man to be holy and righteous before Him forever[27]. Those that follow tenaciously these provisions of the covenant become His holy habitation. This is the anointing of the most holy: the very package designed by God such that when we keep to the terms of this covenant, it will bring an end to our sins, reconcile us to God and instil everlasting righteousness in us.

The lack of this understanding and the fear of our present spiritual decadence have made us fix the anointing of the holy habitation of God in the future after a presupposed future great tribulation. Consequently, some of us now believe that since Jesus the Messiah left the earth, we have been in the period of the remaining one week. It is presumed that we are in the first half of the one week and that after the church is caught up, the tribulation will start and last for another half- week. Others presume that time stopped after Jesus was caught up and will remain like that until the church is caught up then the remaining one week will start and last for seven tribulation years. **Will it be correct for us to use a different yardstick to interpret the first sixty-nine weeks from that of the remaining one week?** Gabriel that interpreted that prophecy to Daniel never gave such indications. Unfortunately, so many of us have based our interpretation of eschatological scriptures on this error.

Of a truth, seventy weeks literally (i.e in man's calendar) is equivalent to four hundred and ninety days. For the fact that the Messiah did not come, neither was he cut off within a literal four hundred and ninety days from the time of the order to restore again Jerusalem; it means that the seventy weeks period is a God–time–coded period. The only land marks to understanding it is that from the time it started to the time the Messiah was cut off constitutes God's time frame of sixty-nine weeks. These land marks we already know started from Cyrus order in about 536 BC, and the Messiah was cut off about AD 31. The remaining one week elapsed immediately after the Messiah was cut off according to the same rate at which the sixty-nine weeks came to pass. It is wrong therefore to have supposed that the remaining one week is yet to be concluded until a presumed future great tribulation begins.

We need to reason together and come to a clear understanding of the truth as the Holy Spirit desires. It is common among Christians in eschatological studies to attribute each person's view to a school of thought. The multiplicity of these schools of thought has compounded our problem leading to much confusion and deception. These two tools– **Deception** and **Confusion** are our enemy's major tools of operation that have worked an unprecedented level of **Destruction** among men and in the camp of the saints.

Thus our enemy has succeeded in deceiving us about the timeframe and implications of this Great Tribulation with myriad schools of thought, making us believe that the issues of the Great Tribulation are still in the future and do not concern us. In this ignorance, negligence and lack of knowledge, we have cast restraint to the winds and are destroyed daily; the house of the Lord has become a den of thieves and a citadel of merchandise with all forms of schisms, rancour, deception, selfishness and worldliness boldly manifest among us. We have become so confused and are independently struggling under the weight of besetting sins, while hoping that someday, somehow we may be able to make it to our blessed hope at Christ's bosom.

It has become necessary to assess and judge ourselves to know how we have fared from God's perspective in this warfare (or great resistance) against all godliness. In the next chapter we will proceed to determine the timings and components of the Great Tribulation.

END NOTES

1. Jer.25:1-12, 29:1-10
2. Jer.29:10-14; 30:3, 15-22; 31:7-9; 32:37-44
3. Jer.30:4-11,15
4. Jer. 29:13-14; 32:37-44
5. Jer.31:27-34, 32: 37-44
6. Jer.31:34
7. Jer.31:33; 32:40
8. Jer.31:23, 35-40, 33:16
9. Jer.30:12-13
10. Dan 9:12,17,18
11. Dan. 9:5
12. Dan 9:15-16
13. Dan 9:16, 19
14. Ezekiel 37:18-28; 43:12 (NIV)
15. Dan.9:24
16. Daniel 9:25-27
17. Matt.24:15
18. 2Chro.36:21
19. Heb.8:7-10, 10:1-18
20. Matt.21:33-43
21. Matt.23:37-39
22. Matt.22:1-14
23. Jn.8:31-36; 1 Jn.3:5-10
24. Heb.8:6-13
25. 1 Jn.3:9
26. Jn.8:30-38
27. 2 Pet.1:3

Chapter Three

3.0 The Timing and Important Features of the Great Tribulation

—⚞—

In chapter two, we mentioned the two main views out of the many we hold in Christendom presently, with respect to the timing of the great tribulation and highlighted their shortcomings. We will in this chapter be looking critically into the accounts of Jesus and John concerning the timings of the great tribulation and the implications of this event.

According to the *Oxford Advanced Learners Dictionary* we have the definition of the following words:

Tribulation: Any event or action that causes great <u>*trouble*</u> or <u>*suffering*</u>.

Trouble: Any situation causing worry, pain, difficulty, danger, dispute, fighting, unrest, illness, affliction or inconvenience.

Suffering: Feelings of pain, unhappiness, discomfort, distress or great sorrow.

Thus, we can define tribulation as any event, action, or situation that causes **great worry, pain, difficulty, danger, dispute, fighting, unrest, illness, affliction or inconvenience** or that causes **great feelings of pain, unhappiness, discomfort, sorrow or distress**.

3.0 The Timing and Important Features of the Great Tribulation

The word 'tribulation' presupposes a significant level of trouble and 'great tribulation' obviously indicates the same thing but with greater severity. To a large extent, the usage of either word depends on the perception of the person trying to describe the event. Both words were used in different scenarios in the scriptures to refer to the same thing. However, the import of the adjective *great* which was used to qualify the word *Tribulation* conveys an enormous degree of severity as a result of peculiar characteristics such as the complexity of the event, the nature of the key players, the intensity of the predicament faced by all men during the event, etc.

Furthermore, the words *great tribulation* is noted to have been used three times in the KJV of the New Testament[1]. A closer look at the implication of its use in these instances will help us to see that it means the same thing as the word tribulation. For instance:

1. In Matthew 24:15-21, it was used under the description of a devastating war with all its consequences of pain, hunger, nakedness, homelessness, discomfort, etc. This has the same implication as the word *tribulation* in which the **'war'** is the event or action that caused all the great trouble or suffering.

2. In Revelation 2:22-23, it was used under the description of pain, death and sorrow. In this case, **'*being cast into a bed of torment*'** is the event that will bring about great suffering.

3. Also, in its use in Revelation 7:13-17, which refers to the main subject of this book, it was used to depict hunger, thirst and all the sorrows under the sun and heat of this world. In this case, the execution of the dragon's **'*great wrath*'** (against all godliness and the inhabitants of the earth) is the event or action that caused men to be evicted out of the Garden of Eden and brought about all the suffering and trouble. Thus, indicating that both words connote the same meaning.

The phrase *great tribulation* as used in the context of Revelation 7:13-17 was interchanged with the word *sorrow* (i.e tribulations) in Revelation 21:4, ***for they both characteristically refer to the same event***. Thus, when the scripture makes mention of the troubles and afflictions of our present world system, it is referring to the great tribulations of this present world, starting from Adam's fall to the second coming of Christ. This tribulation is consequential to the coming to the earth of the dragon and a third of the angels with great wrath against godliness among the earth's inhabitants; and is also consequential to man's handing over of the world's government to the dragon². *On this note, we should realize, that any place the scripture uses the word Tribulation it means the same thing as Great Tribulation and vice-a-versa.*

The record of Revelation 21:4 makes it clear that all these sorrows, pain, hunger and death (*or great tribulation according to* Rev.7:13-17), are the things that constitute and characterize the former things (world system or governments) that will pass away for a new order or world government. *We therefore conclude, that all the sorrows (or tribulations) under this present world system, which things constitutes the dragon's great resistance against all godliness, is what the scriptures here refers to as the Great Tribulation.*

With this background in mind, we shall now consider different accounts concerning the tribulations as proclaimed by Jesus and John.

3.1 JESUS'S ACCOUNT OF THE TRIBULATION FROM THE GOSPELS.

In the records of Matthew 24, Mark 13 and Luke 21, we find the apostles enquiring from Jesus about the following:

1. When shall the temple buildings be destroyed?

2. What shall be the sign of his coming and

3. What shall be the sign of the end of the world?

In answering this question, Jesus began with stressing the fact that so many people will come in His name misleading and deceiving many (wolves in sheep clothing). This is why we were advised to watch, test every teaching/doctrine and test every spirit. We were warned not to imbibe any teaching until we have proved it to be from Christ. He also said, "…you shall hear of wars, rumours of wars…famines, pestilence … These are the beginning of sorrows "(i.e. tribulations).

Since the presence of wars, pestilence, etc. indicates that the tribulation has begun, it then means that we have already seen its beginning judging from the abundance of these things in our present time. If that be the case, since these signs have been with us in this world since the devil took authority over man, it means that the tribulation Jesus is referring to, dates back to Adam's eviction from the Garden of Eden and as he described, would keep increasing in intensity and complexity until his appearing.

Jesus further pointed out that other constituents of this tribulation includes persecutions, the multiplicity of deceivers and the prevalence of iniquity which will cause the love of many to wax cold[3]. He rounded up his response by saying that after this tribulation period, the powers of the heavens shall be shaken, the sun darkened etc, then shall He appear in the heavens in the company of His angels. He shall then send His angels to gather His elect from one end of the heavens to the other.

He referred to Noah's case as how the world would be the day He will come. This means that notwithstanding the powers of the heavens that will be shaken and the distress (or tribulations) of the nations at this time, life would seem to be going on normally, with people eating, drinking, marrying, building, investing, etc. Any extraordinary thing therefore, that may occur during this period, may be explained away by our economists and scientists. Then, suddenly the Son of man shall come at a time we least expected. For this reason Jesus warned believers strongly saying "take heed to yourselves, lest at any time your hearts be overcharged (choked, suffocated) with surfeiting, drunkeness and the cares of this life, so that day come upon you unaware. For as a snare shall it come on all them that dwell on the face of the whole earth"[4]. Thus, *we realize that the tribulation started from the time Adam was evicted out of the Garden of Eden and will reach its crescendo at the end of this world system when our king will come to establish His kingdom. It is this period that was referred to in the Revelation of John as the period of great tribulation*[5].

3.1.1 DESCRIPTIVE IMPRESSION OF JESUS'S ACCOUNT

Jesus gave us a picture of the great resistance through the parable of the sower[6]. In this account, the first set of seeds fell by the road side. These set of people heard the word but it made no meaning to them, neither had they time to consider it for the devil immediately removed it from their hearts. These represent unbelievers for the seeds did not even germinate. The second set of seeds fell on stony ground. They were received with gladness, and germinated, but were not deeply rooted. These people received the word, got born again, even filled with the Holy Ghost, else they wouldn't have been able to start the race. But along the line, just as every man's faith would be tried by the grievous resistant fiery darts of the enemy in this great tribulation, these withered away because they were not deeply rooted in Christ.

The third set of seeds fell among thorns. These represents those who received the word, got born again, filled with the Holy Spirit and were well nurtured and brought up in the knowledge of the truth, but thorns crept in and began to choke them. That notwithstanding they struggled to grow and mature, but these thorns sapped them; they were weights that kept besetting them. The record of the sower about them is that their works were not found perfect. They could not bring forth fruit, as they became choked by thorns. These thorns represent encumbrances such as: deceitfulness of riches cares of this world and lust (strong desires) of other things. This is a picture of the warfare (the great tribulation),we are in; a period of great delusion. The dragon used these strategies described, to resist the saints and all godliness, opposing and exalting himself above all that is called God, sitting in the temple of God showing that himself is also revered and honoured as God. God has however, made a way of escape, out of all these fiery darts that have come upon mankind, so we can overcome and stand before him on the last day without spot, wrinkle or any blemish[7]. This is the case with the fourth set of seeds that fell on good soil. These last group bore fruits to different levels and their fruits *remained unaborted*[8]. But the third group could not bear any fruit. This parable gives us a picture of the great resistance against all godliness that all men (believers and unbelievers) will face on earth. We would see later in details under the nature of the great tribulation (chapter seven) how these fiery darts have been used by the dragon to overcome many Christians in this warfare making most of us come under the third category of the seeds.

3.1.2 FACTS SUPPORTING JESUS'S ACCOUNT

In responding to the question as to the sign that will herald His coming (and our subsequent rapture), Jesus categorically stated that His coming will be *after* the tribulation of those days[9]. A question that comes to mind is: how then did we come about the idea that Jesus will come *before* the great tribulation to rapture us? One wonders how the devil has beclouded the truth of God from us. Jesus sternly warned about deception for four consecutive times in our text. One common factor most men (believers and unbelievers alike) would discover at the end of times is that they have been grossly deceived in so many ways. The prince of this world was rightly described by the angels as the deceiver of the whole world[10].

We have a major problem which stem from the fact that we do not seem to understand the important features and reason behind the Great Tribulation and the nature of this warfare. We have long supposed that it is meant for God's vengeance on the unbelieving. But this is not true! Paul made it clear that God's vengeance is at the appearance of Christ[11] and this was also confirmed by John[12]. If we were not to partake in this tribulation, why will God then have to wipe away tears caused by the effect of the great tribulations from the face of all the people saved from the earth in Revelation 7:16 and 21:1-4. ***The records of Revelation 7:14-17;21:1-4, indicates that the great tribulation consists of all the sorrows(tribulations) under the sun from Adam to Christ's second coming which include hunger, famine, war, distress, etc., corresponding to Jesus's account in Matthew 24:6-8.*** Thus since the fall of man at the garden of Eden, man came under the torment or tribulation of the devil. This tribulation was not designed for God's vengeance on the unbelieving. Every man will rather be tested and proved by these fearsome sorrows and only those who overcome the dragon through this troublesome times will make it to God's kingdom and God will wipe away their tears and pains at the end of times.

Ultimately, the key features of the Great Tribulation include the following: the resistance of the place of God in man, to make them unable to pursue after Christ, to get them to sell their 'birth right' and ultimately surrender to the enemy. Satan's agenda started and will end with an attempt consisting of all activities under the sun that cause pain, crying and sorrow to displace the Almighty God" in the hearts of all men and to steal, kill and destroy them.

3.2 JOHN'S ACCOUNT OF THE TRIBULATION AS RECORDED IN THE BOOK OF REVELATION

At the beginning of this chapter, we made it clear that its purpose is to critically and conclusively deduce from the accounts of Jesus and John, the timing of the Great Tribulation and the implication of this event. Hopefully, we may see the same trend as described in Matthew 24, more explicitly expounded in the book of Revelation.

In Revelation 1:1, John made clear God's purpose for the things contained in the revelations of Christ which were to be recorded (vs. 11) and sent to the seven churches in Asia. He was instructed to write the following[13]:

1. the things which he had seen,

2. the things which are, and

3. the things which shall be thereafter.

Some people believe that Rev. Chapters 1-3 consist of events under points one and two above and represents the church age and that Rev. 4 till the end consists of things to come in the future, simply because John was told to come up to see the things that must be thereafter. We have thus interpreted all the things from Revelation 4 to the end as things that only have to do with the future and as such, do not concern the church. Such interpretation forces us to attach futuristic interpretations on all events and beings mentioned therein, thereby neglecting the fact that some of these events and beings mentioned in Rev.12-18 have been, are, and shall be thereafter. The sectioning of the book of Revelation into chapters and verses was simply to help us organize information and does not necessarily mean that the sequences of events were demarcated by chapters. We assumed a non-identifiable rapture in Revelation 4 and a future rapture after a presumed great tribulation from Revelation 4 to 19. The interpretation of the timing of the Great Tribulation based on this premise is not accurate. We fault the premise of this interpretation on the grounds that the whore and beasts referred to in Rev.12, 13 and 17 have been in operation since the time of Adam. Details of this fact are presented in the subsequent chapters of this book. We conclude therefore that the things that were revealed to John comprised of:

1. the things which have been (revealed under the things which he has seen)

2. the things which are and

3. the things which shall be thereafter.

The overall essence of the book of Revelation to John is to help the church to understand all the issues that relate to our warfare during the Great Tribulation. It unfolds the very great resistance every believer will face on earth. These have been prophesied by Daniel, the prophets of old, Jesus of Nazareth, and the Disciples of Christ. I believe the Lord intends that with such knowledge and understanding, we be equipped to fight the good fight of faith and not be overtaken by the prince of this world. It is for this reason the word "overcome/overcometh" was used not less than eleven times in the book.

Without understanding the Revelation of John, we would not be able to fully appreciate the intricate nature of our warfare. For this reason, those that pay little attention to this book in the Bible or suggest that we can do without it, are playing on a dangerous ground. To show how important it is, God left the responsibility of our making it to His kingdom with us using the following words '… he who wants to overcome, let him overcome….." for He has given us all the necessary information and resources to fight this warfare.

3.2.1 THE PRESUMED RAPTURE OF THE CHURCH BEFORE THE TRIBULATION

Some well-meaning people have asserted that the church will be *raptured* before the events recorded in Revelation 4 and that Christ will come twice. First, His coming in the air to rapture the church; secondly His coming to the earth with the saints to reign. Note that for both cases they presume there will be a resurrection of the dead in Christ. Furthermore they assert that the major difference between the two (His coming and His appearing) are:

1. That in the first He comes for His saints, and in the latter case He comes with the saints.

2. That in the first case He appears in the air, but in the latter case He comes down on earth.

To buttress their points, they have cited various scriptures[14]. In Jesus's account, however, He never mentioned that He was going to come twice, the angels in Acts 1:10-11 didn't give such an indication and we can also not draw such conclusions from the account of John in Revelation 4. John was told to come up to heaven in Rev.4:1 but it will not make sense to pre-suppose that this coincides with the first coming of Christ and the first rapture. There is no evidence in the text to establish this view. On a critical study of the Revelations concerning the coming of Christ; there is no other mention of the coming of Christ in the air or in the world outside the one mentioned in chapter 19, which corresponds to "after the tribulations of those days" and collaborates Jesus's predictions in Matthew 24:29-31.

At the tail end of the tribulation, after that great city which was found to be responsible for all the iniquities committed on earth was judged, the saints on earth were seen to have gotten ready for their wedding to Jesus[15]. They were ready for the wedding, but the rapture had not taken place. This was followed by the appearance of the King of the saints with the armies in heaven from Revelation 19:11. The beast and the false prophet were bound and cast into the lake of fire[16]. The devil was bound and cast into the bottomless pit[17]. This was then followed by the rapture and thereafter marriage (joining or union) of the Lamb to His bride[18]. At the rapture, the dead in Christ will rise first thus, came the fulfilment of 1 Thessalonians 4:16-17. Here the scripture categorically stated that: ***this is the first resurrection***[19] and the angel said blessed and holy is he that hath part in the first resurrection[20]. The second resurrection is for the rest of the dead who did not die in Christ[21].

3.2.2 FACTS SUPPORTING JOHN'S ACCOUNT

1. If the church and the Holy Spirit were to be removed out of the way via the rapture for the Great Tribulation to start (as some of us thought), how then did a great number of believers come out of the Great Tribulation[22]? Their conversion, conviction and sustenance could have only been through the power and presence of the Holy Spirit working on earth and in their lives. Can there be salvation without the Holy Spirit? Some of us in response to these objections presume that these ones may be saved by reason of their own blood. In this regard, we lose sight of the fact that no man shall be considered acceptable before God by the reason of his own blood. Consider this thoroughly and you would see that there has been a major error in pre-supposing that the church and the Holy Spirit will not be on earth during the Great Tribulation.

2. Concerning the 'armies' that came with Jesus in Revelation 19:14, clothed in fine linen white and clean, some of us have erroneously presumed these ones to be the church that must have been *raptured* before this time. *The scriptures made it abundantly clear that Jesus's second coming will be in the company of His angels*[23]. *The scriptures would*

not contradict it-self. The truth therefore is that the armies mentioned therein are angels. These were the same 'armies' that fought in heaven when there was war there[24]. *All these were arraigned in fine linen, clean and white which indicates their holiness.* Jesus made it clear that when we are taken up (at the resurrection), we will be exactly like the angels[25]. The angel in Revelation 19:10 made it clear that we are fellow servants. Our basic outfits shall be the same. The outfit of the angels described in most parts of the scriptures were all the same–white and bright[26]. In some other references[27] the angels were referred to as holy ones, saints, and clothed in linen. We should therefore not be confused to think that sainthood and being clothed with fine white apparel only refer to holy men. It is used in scriptures to also refer to angels. Thus when the scripture said Christ shall come with ten thousands of His saints[28], it was referring to the angels that have kept their first estate.

In the light of the above facts the idea of Christ coming twice after ascension and two resurrections of the dead in Christ, does not hold water. In the light of every other scripture in this respect, this idea will always be found wanting.

We conclude therefore that the Great Tribulation started from the time when the dragon came down to the earth with great wrath and will continue till the time Christ will come with the angels from heaven to take over the kingdoms of the world from the dragon. In the following chapter, we will be looking at the key players in this event and the part they have to play.

END NOTES

    1. Matt.24:21, Rev 2:22 and 7:14 (KJV)
    2. Gen.3:16-17
    3. Matt.24:9-13
    4. Lk.21:34-35
    5. Rev.7:14
    6. Mark 4:2-20
    7. 1 Cor 10:13
    8. Jn.15:16a
    9. Matt.24:29-30, Mark 13:24-27, Lk.21:25-27
    10. Rev.12:9
    11. 2 Thes.1:6-10
    12. Rev.19:11-21

13. Rev.1:19
14. Daniel 12:1-2; 1Thess 4:16-17; Matt. 25:1-13; Rev.20:5; Lk12:40, Matt.25:31-32 & Rev.20:5.
15. Rev.19:7-8
16. Rev.19:20
17. Rev.20:2-3
18. Rev.20:4-6
19. Rev.20:5
20. Rev. 20:6
2. Rev. 20:11-13
22. Rev.7:1-17
23. Matt.13:39, 41,49; 16:27; 24:30-31; 2 Thess.1:7
24. Rev.12:7
25. Matt.22:30
26. Matt.28:2-3, Mark16:5 and Acts1:10, 10:30
27. Daniel 4:23, 8:13, 12:6; Rev.14:10
28. 1 Thes.3:13, Jude 1:14

Section B - Key Players in the Great Tribulation

Chapter Four

4.0 The Contention of the Two Great Cities in the Great Sea (*The Waters*)

The essence of Section B covering chapters four to six of this book, is to enable us understand the key players in our warfare. This entails knowing our enemy; his strengths and strategies etc., that we may know how to best wage this war; demonstrating the victory of our Lord Jesus Christ in order to triumph over our enemy. It is a requirement in the 'act of war' to recognize and review your enemies' strategies and tactics to avoid surprises. In Paul's view, being ignorant of our enemy's devices gives the dragon opportunity to take advantage of us[1].

If we think the strategies of our enemy to weaken Christians are merely the well-known vices of fornication, adultery, bribery, theft and murder, then we have missed it. It goes far deeper; is more deceptive than we can imagine and attacks godliness from various frontiers. We should have a clear perspective of these frontiers if we want to experience victory. Otherwise, how can we say like Jesus, "the prince of this world cometh, but has nothing in me." In military intelligence, it is required that you guard information of your strengths/capabilities and strategic plans in warfare. Our enemy, being the prince of deceit and a master in warfare, knows this and has applied this strategy very well. First, he has succeeded at deceiving and confusing us with various schools of thought and making us believe the Great Tribulation is still in the future and that we will not be part of it. Consequently many saints have dropped their guard and have gradually become subservient to the whims and caprices of our enemy and taken citizenship of this world system without knowing it; all because we do not know the things that constitute this great warfare.

The events of Revelation 12-18 clearly highlighted the intricacies of the Great Tribulation. To unravel the strategies of our enemy, we will start with Revelation 12. Here we see the long set out plan of God to create and rule over all of mankind and the resistance posed by the newly formed dragon's kingdom of darkness. Revelation 12 covers the formative stages of this resistance. In Revelation 13 God gave us the grand plan of the dragon's kingdom and how the dragon will go about this warfare to resist every one that calls upon God on planet earth. The events of Revelation 17-18 and Daniel's revelations all point at expatiating this grand plan of the dragon, detailing the intricate nature of the warfare.

The screen begins to scroll with the presentation of the key players in Revelation 12

And there appeared a great wonder in heaven; a woman clothed with the sun and the moon under her feet and upon her head a crown of twelve stars[2]

Paul identified this woman as Jerusalem and as the "mother of us all" in Galatians 4:26. In other words, this identity symbolizes her as the woman who 'gave birth' to us the righteous seed of the earth. It corresponds to Revelation 12:17b, where the children of this woman were referred to as those that "keep the commandments of God and have the testimony of Jesus Christ". Apostle Paul also called her 'Mount Zion,' the heavenly Jerusalem, the city of the living God, *the mother of us all* and explaining that it is composed of two sets of people; those presently in heaven and those presently on earth[3]. In the full description of the heavenly Jerusalem in Revelation[4] the characteristic sun, moon and twelve stars where correlated to this woman of Rev.12. **We deduce therefore, that the woman in this chapter referred to as the mother of all the righteous seed of the earth [those who through the period of their testimony or life on earth kept God's commandments and the testimony of our Lord Jesus Christ] represents the part of the family of God–the heavenly Jerusalem –here on earth.**

4.0 The Contention of the Two Great Cities in the Great Sea (The Waters)

It is important to recognize at this junction that there are two key players called "great cities" in contention over the inhabitants of the earth;

1. The *"great city"* [5] *or "city of the Living God"* also referred to as the heavenly Jerusalem[6]. She is responsible for (i.e. the mother of) all the righteous seed of the earth[7]. ***She represents the kingdom of God.***

2. That *"great city"* which reigneth over the kings and nations of the earth[8]. She is also referred to as Babylon[9]. She was found to be responsible for (i.e. mother of) all the sins and sinners of the whole world[10] from Adam to the second coming of Christ. ***She represents the kingdom of the dragon.***

Both of these cities in the scriptures are symbolized as women! We will see as we proceed that while the seed of the woman of Revelation 12 faced great tribulation within God's coded time frame of one thousand, two hundred and sixty days, the other woman of Revelation 17 and 18 is the one responsible for the great tribulation lasting for exactly the same time frame. ***The battle ground is the great sea (i.e. waters) representing all mankind from Adam till the second coming of Christ***[11].

The rendition in Revelation[12] shows the woman (heavenly Jerusalem) about to deliver a child destined to rule the nations with an iron rod, and the devil positioning himself to devour the child once born. Afterwards, the woman delivered the child who was snatched up to God. When the devil discovered that he could not reach the child, he went after the woman to torment her, but she was also withdrawn out of the devil's reach for a period of one thousand, two hundred and sixty days (forty-two months or three and a half years). At this point, there was another interjection in the trend of the story to show how the dragon came into the picture.

Prior to this event, Lucifer was said to have been resident in heaven. However, he was thrown down when iniquity was found in him, after Michael, supported by two-thirds of the angels fought Lucifer and the rest of the angels[13]. At the point the devil was thrown down, the woman was already in labour[14]. Then he set himself to destroy the child as soon as he was born. Not being able to get at the child, he set his terror against the woman, but God prevented him.

The dragon and his cohorts vexed at this loss, then organized themselves into a kingdom (or great city) referred to as MYSTERY BABYLON; for the sole purpose of resisting the interest of God in man – for with great wroth he set his army against all the seed of the woman[15]. The angels, aware of this impending resistance, predicted terror for all inhabitants of the earth during the period that the dragon and his cartel will legitimately co-inhabit the earth with them. With great fury therefore, the dragon set his city to steal, kill and destroy all of mankind; greatly resisting the place and interest of God in them; pending the time they will be bound not to hurt or deceive the nation's again[16]. ***This period of the dragon's co-inhabitation of the earth with mankind is the period referred to in the scriptures as the period of the Great Tribulation (or great resistance against all godliness), after which Christ will come to take over the kingdoms of the world from the dragon.***

It is pertinent to recognize at this juncture that God withdrew the woman from the reach of the dragon in Rev. 12:14 for a time, times and half a time. This is the same period referred to in Rev.12:6 showing that it is also equal to one thousand, two hundred and sixty days. But there was another part of the woman that God did not withdraw out of the reach of the devil. These are the rest of the woman's offspring – those who keep the commandments of God and hold the testimony of Jesus Christ. These are the ones who, along with all the other inhabitants of the earth[17], faced the fury of the devil for a time, as the angels proclaimed: "woe unto the inhabitants of the earth for the devil is come unto you having great wrath".

> *So then the dragon was furious (enraged) at the woman and he went away to wage war on the remainder of her descendants (on those who obeyed God's commandment and who have the testimony of Jesus Christ and adhere to it and bear witness to him)[18].*

At this point, we would like to observe the following concerning the tenure of the resistance:

1. The short time the dragon has to vex his fury against the children of this woman (heavenly Jerusalem) is the same period for which the woman is to be in the wilderness.

2. The woman was to be in the wilderness according to Rev.12:6 for one thousand, two hundred and sixty days (i.e forty-two months). This is also equated to time and times and half a time in Rev.12:14

3. Rev.13 describes how the dragon went about the resistance against the children of this woman and the tenure of this resistance was clearly

4.0 The Contention of the Two Great Cities in the Great Sea (The Waters)

specified in Rev.13:5 as forty-two months. This collaborates with numbers one and two above.

4. In the records of Dan.12:6-7, the angel while answering how long the kingdoms of this world would be under the prince of the air before Jesus takes it over said it shall be for a time, times and half. This collaborates with the tenure of the great resistance as stated in two and three above. It also portrays the fact that the reign of the four-beasts of Daniel or seven–headed beast of John is what entirely constitutes the **Indignation[19] or Great Tribulation[20] or expression of the wrath of the dragon[21]**. These words were used by different personalities in scripture to refer to the same event.

5. It is within this time frame that the devil will vex all his fury on the inhabitants of the earth starting from Adam and more especially against them that seek righteousness with God and against everything that is called God or God's. During this time, the devil will attempt to exalt his throne above the stars of God and visit devastation upon God's congregation. The records of Dan.12:7b confirms that the essence of the dragon ruling over the four Beasts of Daniel (World Governments) is to fight, resist and accomplish to scatter the power of the holy people.

6. This is the period of man's great sorrow as identified in Gen.3:17-19; also referred to in Rev.7:14 as the period of 'the Great Tribulation.'

We conclude at this juncture that the Great Tribulation is the exercise of the Great Wrath of the Dragon against all the inhabitants of the earth and most especially against the saints (who keep the commandments of God and the testimony of our Lord Jesus Christ). Revelation 13 is a descriptive chapter, showing how the dragon executed this war against the seed of the woman and all the inhabitants of the earth. It was designed to enable them (the seed of the woman) understand the strategies the dragon would employ in resisting them. In a nut shell; it should help us know how the dragon would use the seven–headed beast, the false prophet (and in general all the members of His kingdom –*Mystery Babylon*) to execute the **"GREAT TRIBULATION"** by:

- Vexing his wrath[22]
- Treading underfoot[23]
- Trampling upon[24]
- Sitting[25]

- Fighting against[26]
- Scattering[27]

the elect of God and of Christ on earth. The combined effect of this stampede on the saints is weariness, exhaustion, fatigue, disillusionment and ultimately a loss of our first love for Christ.

END NOTES

1. 2 Cor.2:11
2. Rev.12:1
3. Heb.12:22-24
4. Rev.21:23
5. Rev.21:10
6. Heb.12:22
7. Gal.4:26, Rev.12:17
8. Rev.17:18
9. Rev.18:21
10. Rev.17:5
11. Rev.17:15
12. Rev 12:2-6
13. Rev.12:7-9
14. Rev.12: 2-4
15. Rev.12:17
16. Rev.20:3
17. Rev.12:12
18. Rev.12:17,AV
19. Dan.8:19
20. Rev.7:14
21. Rev.12:17
22. Rev.12:17
23. Rev.11:2 and Dan 8:13
24. Dan.7:7,19, 21
25. 2 Thess.2:4
26. Rev.13:7
27. Dan.12:7

Chapter Five

5.0 Enter ...The Dragon (Rev. 13)

The intent here is to understand how the dragon went about this warfare; opposing and exalting himself above all that is called of God, sitting and trampling upon the temple of God[1] for the period of one thousand, two hundred and sixty days (forty-two months, or time, times and half a time). We will study John's record in Rev.13, correlating it with Revelation 17 and 18 and Daniel's records in Daniel 2, 7 and 8. In the previous chapter, we tried to show how the warfare started and the introduction of the key players. In this chapter, we shall see the formations of the dragon as he fully enters the arena and how his team is organized with specific roles in executing the warfare. Against this backdrop, we will be able to understand what the beasts represent, as this will help us better appreciate our warfare and the tribulations of our time.

5.1.1 JOHN'S ACCOUNT

John, in Rev.13:1-2 and Rev.17:7-11 presents these beasts as kings or kingdoms that rule over the world. They were seen in Rev.17 as the ones carrying the city – Mystery Babylon. Remember that in the last verse of Rev.12, the dragon was vexed with wrath and went to war against the children of the heavenly Jerusalem on earth for a period of forty-two months. To execute this mission, the dragon gave all his power, seat and great authority to the seven-headed beast[2] and another beast called the false prophet[3], to war against the saints for this period of forty-two months[4]. Thus these two beasts constitute the major instruments of warfare for the dragon throughout the period of the Great Tribulation.

The scriptures here clearly identify these kingdoms to be direct replicas of the dragon. In the physical, they were expressed as world kingdoms under physical kings, but in their true forms, they are fallen angels enforcing their powers as beastly principalities in charge of the whole world. This was what made the prophets refer to the kings of Babylon and Tyrus as Lucifer in various accounts[5]. Daniel 10:13 also depicts the same thing.

Meanwhile, it will be proper for us to recognize at this point that, if not for the 'revelation' God gave us through John; it would have been difficult for anyone to fully understand the implications of Daniel's prophecies. Today, the spiritual implications of Daniel's revelations are not well appreciated, but are seen as mere prophetic and historical records of world kingdoms. Both books mirror each other for full comprehension. Unfortunately, they seem to be the least understood books of the Bible.

5.1.2 DANIEL'S ACCOUNT

In Dan.7:1-28, these four great beasts that rose out of the great sea represent four kingdoms ruled by kings according to the interpretation given to him vs.17. These are four major nations (or world governments) that rule over the whole world and will continue till the time Christ will come to set up His kingdom[6] (i.e *till the kingdoms of this world become the kingdoms of His Christ and He shall reign–with His saints– forever and ever* [7]). Notice that the four beasts in this vision symbolize the same world kingdoms that were pictured by the image of Nebuchadnezzar in Daniel 2 and the ten horns of the last beast are the same as the ten toes of the image. While unveiling the first beast in Daniel 2:37-38, Daniel spoke to Nebuchadnezzar and said:

You, o king are the king of kings, to whom the God of heaven has given the kingdom, the power, the strength and the glory,

And where ever the sons of men dwell, or the beast of the field, or the birds of the sky, he has given them into your hand and has caused you to rule over them all. You are the head of gold [8].

In other words, all the kingdoms of the world wherever men dwell, all its glory, power, strength and dominion have been committed to his charge. Thus, he was to rule over all the nations. His kingdom –Babylon–was the first great beast with the resemblance of a lion in Daniel 7. The record of Jeremiah 5:15, indicates that this nation had been from ancient times. *(Bear in mind however, that the real personality behind this kingdom is the prince of the power of the air over Babylon).* After, the reign of this kingdom, the second great beast looking like a bear took over the kingdoms of the whole earth. In Daniel 2, it was likened to silver and was rightly identified in Daniel 5:28 as the Medo-Persian kingdom. A third kingdom likened to brass in Daniel 2 and to a leopard in Daniel 7 took over the kingdoms of the world. The transition events were plainly depicted in Daniel 8. In Daniel 7:6, it was made clear that this third kingdom had four heads which in Daniel 8:8 where referred to as four notable horns. Gabriel in Daniel 8:21-22, went further to explain who these four heads represent.

And the rough goat is the king (or kingdom) of Grecia, and the great horn that is between his eyes is the first king: Now that being broken, whereas four stood up for it four kingdoms shall stand up out of the nation but not in his power [9].

Thus, the Grecian kingdom shall be broken into four other kingdoms: one to the east, one to the west, one to the north and another to the south[10]. This was followed by the last of the four kingdoms referred to as iron, and as a mixture of iron and clay[11], dreadful and exceedingly strong[12]. This beast we all know from historical records to be the Roman kingdom to whom the kingdoms and dominion and the greatness of the kingdom under the whole heaven shall be given until the second coming of Jesus, the great King of all kings, when the kingdom of this world will become the kingdoms of our Lord[13].

5.1.3. CORRELATION OF JOHN'S AND DANIEL'S ACCOUNTS

To correlate these revelations of John and Daniel, it will be wise at this point to recognize that most of the physical features of the beasts identified in Daniel's revelations (as lion, bear and leopard) also featured in the beast of John's revelation[14]; signifying that these beasts refer to the same personalities.

REVELATIONS ON THE NATIONS THAT WILL BEAR RULE OVER THE WORLD

Nebuchadnezzar's dream of major world kingdoms that shall rule before the kingdom of Christ is established on earth.	Daniel's Revelation of 4 major kingdoms that shall rule over the earth before the rule of the Most High	John's revelation of seven kingdoms that shall rule over the earth before the coming of Christ.
GOLD	BABYLON (LION)	FIRST HEAD
SILVER	MEDO – PERSIA (BEAR)	SECOND HEAD
BRASS	GRECIA (LEOPARD), Grecian West (Thrace and Macedonia),	THIRD HEAD
	Grecian North (Syria),	FOURTH HEAD
	Grecian South (Egypt),	FIFTH HEAD
	Grecian East (Seluceid/Parthia)	SIXTH HEAD
IRON (with ten toes)	ROME (Indescribable beast with ten horns)	SEVENTH HEAD (with ten horns).

As at the time of this revelation to John (about AD 90), the first five beasts had finished their dominion over the kingdoms of the earth[15]. The sixth beast was still in operation, but was finally overtaken by the seventh beast under the reign of Emperor Trajan, during a war that raged from AD 114–115 [16]. From then on, this last beast (kingdom) exercised dominion over the world governments. In the course of time, this same kingdom of Iron transmogrified into a mixture of iron and clay within its ten toes, but retained in this complex structure the strength of iron. It will hold on to the dominion over the world governments till the King of kings comes and the Ancient of Days hands over the whole kingdom (governments) under the heavens to Him and His saints[17].

5.2 THE SEVEN HEADED BEAST

The seven–headed beast represents the major kingdoms of the world that shall rule the entire world from the time of Adam to Christ's second coming[18]. In Revelation 13:1, we were informed that the seven–headed beast rose out of the sea, corresponding to Daniel 7:3 in which the four beasts came up out of the sea. In Revelation 17:1, John was told to come and see the judgment of the great whore *"that sits upon many waters."* In verse 3, when he saw this great whore, she was rather sitting upon the seven–headed beast! It appeared as if the beast and the waters could not be separated. The sight was therefore, as though the seven–headed beast encompassed the waters that the woman was sitting on. These same *waters* in Revelation 17:15 were referred to as peoples, multitudes, tongues and nations. The scope of the *waters* was further highlighted in Revelation 13:7 and 14:8 to encompass *all kindred, all tongues, all peoples and all nations that dwell on earth*. Furthermore, the records of Revelation 13:8, 17:6 and 18:24 imply that these "people and nations" mentioned refers to all the people that shall live from Adam to the second coming of Christ whose names were not written in the Lamb's book of life and all the nations that shall thrive on the earth from Adam to Christ's second coming. Thus we conclude that:

1. The seven–headed beast signifies the major kingdoms (governments) that shall bear rule over the inhabitants of the world from its inception to the end.

2. It also symbolizes all the inhabitants of the world that were brought under the government of the whore from Adam till the second coming of Christ. These are the ones identified with the mark of the beast, whose names were not written in the Lamb's book of life from the very foundation of the world to its end.

3. But more particularly, he is a single entity; a fallen angel called the beast, as indicated in Revelation 19:20.

As at the time of this revelation to John, the first-five heads had finished their dominion over the nations[15]. This is a very clear indication that this seven-headed beast has been in operation well before this time and is not a kingdom or king or being that is to come in a pre-supposed future great tribulation as is presently assumed in Christendom.

In the accounts of Rev.13, it was not shown clearly how this seven-headed beast will wage war against all godliness. However, Rev.13:1 says this beast has a name "Blasphemy" written boldly on each of the seven heads of the beast. Blasphemy by inference simply means *irreverence, violence and resistance against God*. In the account of Dan.7:21, we saw this beast making war with the saints and prevailing against them for the same period of time, times and half a time (i.e three and a half years, or forty-two months or one thousand, two hundred and sixty days). This name *Blasphemy* is his essence; depicting his indignation against the saints.

The records of Daniel refer to the reign of this seven–headed beast as a period of indignation[19], war and desolation[20]. *Indignation is wrath,* and consists of resentment, displeasure, animosity, anger, vexation, exasperation, tribulations, etc. These are the things that constitute *the great wrath* of the dragon against the inhabitants of the earth and more especially against the holy ones[21]. *The expression of this great wrath is what constitutes the Great Tribulation. The dragon will execute this indignation (or Great Tribulation) via the seven–headed beast from Adam to the second coming of Christ.* The details and intricate nature of this warfare were not shown in Daniel's revelations, but was clearly demonstrated through the false prophet of the beast in Rev.13.

5.3 THE FALSE PROPHET OF THE 7-HEADED BEAST

In Rev.13:11-18 we see another beast with horns like a lamb, rising up out of the earth and identified with another name in Rev.19:20 as the "false prophet." This beast is generally referred to in Christendom as the Antichrist.

To further identify the sphere and tenure of the operations of this second beast, we will take a closer look at Rev.13:12, 14. In verse 12, we discover that this second beast exercised all the powers of the first beast. Now let's outline all the powers of the first beast as earmarked in Rev.13:

Verse 2: he was given all the dragon's power, seat and great authority

Verse 5: he was given power to continue (war against the saints and inhabitants of the earth) for 42 months. We have previously clearly identified this period as stemming from the beginning of the world to the second coming of Christ.

Verse 7-8: he was given power over ALL kindred, tongues, peoples and ALL nations that dwell and will dwell upon the earth.

This scope of authority (power) clearly identifies the first beast's scope of authority. It is this same scope of authority that was given to the second beast[22]. Thus, this second beast's tenure of operation (according to verse 5) is also from the beginning of the world to the end when Christ will establish His own kingdom over the world. This implies that we were wrong to have

5.0 Enter ...The Dragon (Rev. 13)

thought in Christendom that this false prophet (*also called the Antichrist*) is to come in the future. These verses indicate that he worked hand-in-hand with the seven–headed beast that had been from Adam and will continue till the second coming of Christ. One may think that since the first and second beasts are to operate exactly the same power of the dragon that they may conflict. But Rev.13:14 and Rev.19:20 made it clear that the second beast officiated as a lieutenant, and a prophet to the first beast, and will exercise its mandate in the very presence of the seven-headed beast.

It is through this false prophet that the intricate nature of the indignation (or Great Tribulation) was clearly demonstrated. From Rev.13:13 downwards, John was summarily shown the activities (vices) of the false prophet under two major subjects:

1. Idolatry (and sorcery) and
2. World Commerce

It is probably these two strategies that constitute the two horns of this beast. It is important to note at this point that the horn of a beast (or animal) represents the fighting instrument of the beast. We should not forget that just as the whore (the dragon's kingdom of darkness) is expressed through the seven–headed beast, so is she also expressed through this lieutenant–the false prophet. As a matter of fact, this false prophet seems to focus his power in enforcing the whore's two major vices. Let us now expatiate on these vices of the false prophet:

1. IDOLATRY (AND SORCERY)

Rev.13:13-14 shows that the false prophet wielded so much power with signs and wonders following all his acts. He initiated idolatry on earth. He was the brain behind the order that those who did not worship or bow to the image of the beast should be killed[23]. We have reason to believe that one of the heads of the beast that was wounded by the sword but later healed represents Nebuchadnezzar of Babylonian kingdom. This happened when God wanted to show the whore and all the inhabitants of the earth that though the prince of this world rules over the earth, that He (God) rules over and above all of them and gives the kingdom to whomsoever He wills. After the wound healed, instead of men fearing God, this false prophet turned their hearts to fear the prince behind Nebuchadnezzar and to worship him all the more rather than worship God. The false prophet inspired them to make images unto the prince of Babylon and ordered all the inhabitants of the world to bow down to this image, declaring that whosoever did not should be killed. The false prophet has continued in this bid over the years, practicing this vice through the reign of the seven heads of the beast. He stood by the kings of the nations to advise them to destroy anyone who did not bow to their national images, declaring them to be heretics; non-conformists and disloyal.

Throughout the history of human civilization this false prophet employed the services of magicians, sorcerers and those involved in occultism, to be the advisers of the kings of the nations. The records of history show that through this means, the nations where held spellbound to the whims and caprices of the dragon and were thereby given to idolatry and sorcery. It was through him that the whore greatly enforced her sorcery and idolatry over all the nations of the earth and its influence was so overwhelming and practices so successful, that before the first coming of Christ all nations of the earth–excluding some Jews–were under this strong delusion. We do not intend to start delving into details of how idolatry and sorcery have been extensively and sophisticatedly practiced in today's world. Many books have been written on the subject. However what is frightening now is the extent to which sorcery and idolatry has crept into modern day churches and so many believers have been deceived.

2. WORLD COMMERCE

This vice of the false prophet is rather the most deceitful and has been used to overcome so many and to bring them under the web of the whore. To understand this better, let us take a closer look at Rev.13:16 and 17 and note the word *all*. Who are these "all"? They represent all that dwell on earth through the tenure of the beast's operation (which is from Adam to Christ's second coming), who through the period of their lives, lived under the government or influence of the whore. In these verses we see this false prophet enforcing the second vice of the whore upon all the inhabitants of the earth; setting up a world system where it will be very difficult for anyone to buy or sell except the person has the mark of the beast. Everything we do on earth to acquire or obtain food, clothing and shelter all come under the canopy of buying and selling–*merchandize*. The extent to which men have today become captivated with these pursuits rather than attend to God, demonstrates the success of the enemy with this strategy. Meanwhile, the scripture makes it clear that these pursuits are the ways of the gentiles which lead to eternal death–*because, the person we devote ourselves to, is the one we are serving*[24]. These systems have been designed by the dragon such that when we are set after them, we are set after his kingdom (the whore) and thereby identifying with the mark of his beast.

It is so easy to miss the fact that the scripture did not say 'no body will be able to buy or sell without the mark, but that nobody *might* be able to buy or sell. Thus, some people might still be able to buy or sell without taking this mark[25]. These are the overcomers, the elect few that shall escape the beast's plan and go through all these things and stand victorious before Christ in the day of the Lord. The activities of the whore, as seen in the scriptures, were effectively implemented through the false prophet via his position as the special adviser and prophet to the kings of the nations (the world governments). We will explain further in the following chapters how these vices apply in our modern world systems and have led to many Christians compromising their stand with Christ.

Our major concern at this point is this: seeing that the false prophet (or Antichrist) has been in operation since the time of Adam, how then does the giving of the mark of the beast apply? A mark could be described as an inscription or sign. Any mark, seal, sign, number or name is intended to authentically identify the bearer. Every human being born into the world has a given name meant to identify him or her at any point in time. Thus, this wisdom behind giving a name is the same behind giving a mark – *identification, and in some instances, allegiance and ownership.* The mark of the beast identifies the presence, person, authority, lordship or influence of the beast over them that bear it at any point in time. It simply identifies the bearer as belonging to the beast.

Many Christian writers have expressed their views regarding the mark of the beast which Rev.13:18 clarifies as being the number of a name, furthermore the number of a man *666*. The objective of this book is not to dispute some of the well thought-out explanations but to help each Christian understand that ***the bottom line is that this mark is for identification and the beast that is controlling the world commerce with it has been in operation since the existence of man.***

We recognize that from the beginning of creation, all the representatives of the whore have been used by her to entice, force and compel people to participate in her vices, such as: sin, idolatry, sorcery, materialism, etc. On the other hand, God has done everything necessary to bring His kingdom down to men and to persuade all men to partake of His divine nature. Remember that in any contest, each contestant is made to appear in an outfit different from the opponent's, for identification. There are two sides to this great conflict we have been discussing – good and evil – each having separate peculiar marks of identification. Let us consider this reference in scripture:

> ... Nevertheless, the foundation of God standeth sure, having this SEAL, the Lord knoweth them that are his. And let everyone that nameth (or beareth, or is identified with) the name (seal, sign or mark) of Christ depart from iniquity[26].

This verse points to the fact that, throughout the period of human existence on earth, ***iniquity*** has been used as the mark that identifies the people in the camp of the dragon; and ***righteousness (departing from iniquity)*** is the mark that identifies the people in the camp of Christ[27]. Thus, we can safely infer that every man is either bearing the mark of Christ or the mark of the beast right now, because both are in operation and the two kingdoms are in a contest over the souls of men from the beginning of time till Christ comes.

While not categorically disputing the fact that it is possible for there to be a progression toward giving of physical marks, "***Iniquity***" is a mark being given in the spirit realm to enable anyone who receives it to survive in the world. Thus, the dragon has so designed this world system under him in such a way that the saints can hardly survive without taking his mark. For this reason the Lord enjoined his elect to come out of her (the whore) and not be conformed to this world. To ensure that those people in His camp are enabled to retain His identity, God invested His Holy Spirit in them as a ***seal***[28]. This seal is not usually identified with the physical eyes, but its influence can be seen. It is this seal (the Holy Spirit) that now leads them through all paths of righteousness, making them depart from iniquity and unfolding the character or ***identity*** of the owner of the temple through the very ***fruits*** they bear. ***The only consistently visible part of these mark, name or seal is the very fruit that men bear. This is the reason Jesus said "... by their fruits, ye shall know (identify) them". In other words, the ownership can be ascertained by the individual's fruit.*** Consequently, when a man bears the mark of the beast, he easily makes merchandize and a living out of it, but when he bears the mark of righteousness, it becomes more difficult for him to make a living out of this world system.

From the forgoing we have seen how the battle has been drawn and the dragon has cunningly shrouded his strategies under a very deceptive covering using two major operational beasts to execute his wrath against the saints. For this reason, the bible refers to the dragon's camp as MYSTERY, BABYLON. In our next chapter, we will critically examine the person and devices of the great

5.0 Enter ...The Dragon (Rev. 13)

whore and her inter-relationship with the seven–headed beast and the false prophet. Also we will identify the intricate workings of the dragon and how he employs and deploys these principalities against the saints. This book is not intended to vilify the enemy but that the saints may know how complex, deceptive and determined our opponent is and to recognize his many-sided strokes. Otherwise we will be fighting amidst a smoke screen of confusion not knowing where the enemy's darts are coming from, thus making us vulnerable.

END NOTES

1. Is. I4:13, 14, 17; 2 Thes.2:4, Rev.11:1-2
2. Rev.13:2
3. Rev.13:12
4. Rev.13:5
5. Is.14:3-12, Ez.28:11-19
6. Dan.7:13-14,
7. Rev.11:15
8. Dan.2:37-38, NASV
9. Dan.8:21-22
10. Dan.8:8)
11. Dan.2:33
12. Dan.7:7
13. Dan.7:27, Rev.11:15
14. Rev.13:2
15. Rev.17:10
16. American Encyclopedia, vol. 23, p. 727; Public Broadcasting Service, USA *"The Roman Empire in the 1st Century"*
17. Dan.7:22;
18. Dan.7:17-18
19. Dan.8:19
20. Dan. 9:27
21. Rev.12:12, 17
22. Rev.13:12
23. Dan.3:4-6
24. Matt.6:32
25. Rev.14:9-13, Rev.20:4-5
26. 2 Tim.2:19 *paraphrased*
27. 1 John 3:8-10
28. Eph. 1:13; 4:30; 2 Cor.1:22

Chapter Six

6.0 Introducing the Great Whore (Mystery Babylon)

It has become absolutely necessary to explain who and what Mystery Babylon represents and her inter-relationship with the dragon, the seven-headed beast and the false prophet, as this will go a long way in helping us to understand the nature of the Great Tribulation. Our enemy has thus far strategically kept her true identity and devices from being understood by God's people. Thus in our misconceptions and misunderstandings of this mysterious personality, she has accomplished her essence of deceiving and destroying many unnoticed, regardless of the fact that God has given us all the necessary information and tools to understand and withstand her.

It is my earnest prayer as we proceed in this extensive exposition of the great whore, that God will open our understanding to His own perspective of this great and well organized city, to the end that we may understand the intricacies of the warfare we are involved in under this great tribulation and extricate ourselves from her grip by the power of the Holy Spirit.

In Rev.17 and 18, John was given a comprehensive insight into the personality and manner of operation of the whore, and her inter-relationship with the seven-headed beast. In Rev.17:3 the whore was seen as sitting upon and being carried by the seven-headed beast. This implies that the whore incubates, saddles and moves the seven-headed beast and that the seven headed beast is her seat or throne and base from where she is expressed. In short, this implies that the kingdom of darkness rests upon the seven headed beast. This is an indication that though in Rev.13 it seemed the seven–headed beast operated independently, yet he was according to this context, invisibly and directly saddled and propelled by the whore. It is consistent with the fact that in Rev.13 the dominion exercised by this seven-headed beast was that of the dragon. In terms of her role and essence Rev.17:5 identified the whore as the mother– source, incubator and initiator of all the abominations (sins and iniquity) committed on earth. This verse clearly posited her personality in three major formats:

- **MYSTERY,**
- **BABYLON THE GREAT,**
- **THE MOTHER OF HARLOTS AND ABOMINATIONS OF THE EARTH**

MYSTERY: In the University Roger's Thesaurus; *invisible, uncertain, obscure, concealed, crafty, and secret* are words that describe the use of the word *mystery*. No wonder, today she is so misconceived and the truth behind her personality has been concealed by her. She is so crafty and has therefore deceived and is destroying man due to the obscure nature of her personality. She is the bedrock of deceit.

BABYLON THE GREAT: She is the invisible and great city beyond man's physical sight, which rules over all the inhabitants of the earth with the exception of the elect. This is the kingdom of the Anti-Christ ruling over all the governments of the world that have been, that are, and shall yet be until Christ takes over the kingdoms of the world.

THE MOTHER OF HARLOTS AND ABOMINATIONS OF THE EARTH: She is the mother (i.e the one who gave birth to or is responsible for the initiation, design, introduction and enforcement) of all the ***abominations*** (sins, sorcery, idolatry, etc) committed by the inhabitants of the earth from Adam to Christ as recorded in the Bible. She caused all the inhabitants of the earth to commit these abominations (fornications) with her and for this reason they were called harlots.

If in God's assessment and Revelation of Christ, He calls this city *'great'*, then there is something characteristically exceptional about this city which He considers as a direct opposite to His own city (Jerusalem), and the saints need to watch and tread carefully. This city is also a kingdom, symbolized as the whore and *is made up of the dragon himself, the seven–headed beast, the false prophet, all other fallen angels also known as principalities and powers (demons), hell and death, the souls of unjust men who have passed to the great beyond, and the unbelieving or unrighteous (referred to in Revelation 11:2 as gentiles). The dragon is the captain of this great city. In other words, the whore symbolizes the kingdom of the dragon (or the kingdom of the world) while the Dragon remains the god or grand commander of this.*

Mystery Babylon is obviously an organized city with its hierarchal order. Just as the case of Jerusalem described as *the mother of all the righteous ones of the earth*, Mystery Babylon is the mother of all unrighteousness, and of all the unrighteous ones in the world. She is also referred to as the great city that ruled and still rules over *all* the nations of the earth (i.e. all the governments of the world from Adam to Christ's second coming[1]). In other words, she has been directly in charge of all the governments of the world; seating on them, compelling and initiating their actions, decrees, and ordinances. She directly propelled these governments and kings of the earth. In Rev.17:6 the blood of all the saints and martyrs of Jesus were found in her. She masterminded their slaughter through the beast. *A quick reference to Rev.18:24 shows that she was responsible also for the blood of all the people that were slain from the foundation of the world to its end (i.e from Abel to the last man that shall die on earth)*. Therefore, she is not a city that is yet to be in future as we presently presume, but a city that has been from creation. She initiated all the wars, pestilence, diseases, hunger; tribulations, that have been from the Garden of Eden, to simply steal, kill and destroy man. This picture painted here of this city clearly depicts that from the foundation of the world, *she was* and will continue to operate with increasing intensity of tribulations till the second coming of Christ.

Till date, many of us have thought that this Babylon is a city that shall emerge in the future. These scriptures however depict her as an all-time city, an organized kingdom (like the kingdom of Christ) beyond man's physical sight that has been from the beginning of the earth. She is responsible for all the iniquities committed on earth, and will continue to ruler over the world governments and the inhabitants of the world until the coming of Christ to take over the kingdoms of the world. This whore will continue to reign over the world system for the period of forty-two months which the dragon has to vex his fury on all the inhabitants of the earth as proclaimed by the angel in Revelation 12:17 and 13:5. This period is also referred to as one thousand, two hundred and sixty days; or a time, times and half a time[2]. This timing that stems from Adam to the end of this world system at the second coming of Christ should not be confused with man's timing. Our conclusion on this in chapter two of this book is that 'time' with God is different from what it is with man.

6.1 THE NATURE OF THE WHORE'S ACTIVITIES

Harlotry or whoredom suggests some form of enticement with promises of pleasure. The whore has employed this strategy to bring all the inhabitants of the earth under her. The intricate details of the activities of the whore were spelt out in Rev.18 in the course of her judgment. In Rev.18:3, the angel summarized the whore's vices and offences under two segments:
- She caused all nations, peoples, and kings (all the inhabitants[3]) of the earth to commit fornication with her (further explained in Rev.18:23c as **sorceries** and earlier in Revelation 17:4 as **abominations**). She was thereby referred to as *the mother of all abominations of the earth*[4].
- The *world system with its commerce* was founded (initiated) and nurtured (sustained) by her. Consequently, immediately after God's judgment was declared on her and she was burnt and destroyed, the world commerce and world systems collapsed[5].

At this point, we will examine in full details the activities (vices) of this WHORE under the two areas mentioned above.

6.2. THE WHORE AS THE MOTHER, INITIATOR, SOURCE OR BRAIN BEHIND ALL THE ABOMINATIONS ON EARTH

To uncover all the abominations that were committed on earth as recorded in scriptures, there were two major classes of abominations that the inhabitants of the earth have been guilty of.

(A) SIN (INIQUITY) OTHER THAN SORCERIES

All forms of sin, iniquity, or unrighteousness committed by *all the inhabitants of the earth were abominations* directly initiated and influenced by the whore. Such instances are seen in:
- Proverbs 3:32, the froward (perverse, wayward, etc.) is considered to be committing an abomination.

- Proverbs 16:5, the proud at heart is considered to be committing an abomination.
- Deuteronomy 25:16; ALL that are involved in unrighteousness are considered to be committing abominations.

(B) SORCERIES (IDOLATORY) REFERRED TO AS THE ABOMINATION OF THE HEATHENS

(i) **IDOLATRY**: The whore is behind the introduction and worship of idols among all the inhabitants of the earth. The graven images are abominations to the Lord[6]. These things include all the idols of the nations of *all* peoples that have been and will be on the face of the earth e.g.
- the goddess Ashtoreth; referred to as the abominations of the Sidonians[7]
- the god Chemosh; referred to as the abominations of the Moabites[7]
- the god Milcom (Molec); referred to as the abominations of the Ammonites[7]
- the goddess Diane; referred to as the abominations of the Ephesians[8]

These also include the worship of the sun, the planets (the constellations of the Zodiac and all the hosts of heaven[9]). She was the brain behind all these abominations committed by the inhabitants of the earth.

(ii) **SORCERY**: All forms of sorcery practiced by the inhabitants of this world–past, present and in the future – were abominations designed, introduced and sustained by the whore. For this reason, the Lord said in Deut.18:9-12, you shall not do after the abominations of the nations which things include:
- Passing your sons and daughters through the fire and human sacrifice.
- Using divinations, forecasting of the future through supernatural means.
- Observing times (astrology, horoscope, etc), the art of studying the position of the stars and its movement to influence human affairs.
- Enchantments: the use of magic spells from anywhere including the marine world.
- Witchcraft: the use of magic to influence and to hurt, control or manipulate others.
- Charms: the use of magic powers, transcendental mediations, etc.
- Magic: the art of controlling events by use of supernatural forces.
- Ventriloquism: consulting with familiar spirits.
- Necromancy: communication with the dead (spirits) to learn about the future.

In summarizing this first vice of the Whore, **we find her as being responsible for all the iniquities and sorceries that were and shall be committed by the inhabitants of the earth**. From the time of Adam she started introducing iniquity and the idea of personal gods for the purpose of displacing God. She masterminded the introduction of sin and wickedness to all the inhabitants of the earth. To this end, God commented in the first few years of man's creation that man's wickedness is great and every imagination of his heart is continually evil[10]. As men multiplied on earth she multiplied these abominations causing them to commit more grievous iniquities and to extend the boundaries of idolatry and sorcery to family, kindred, city, national and international levels. It was the norm and way of life of all past civilizations. She has gone further through her cohorts to develop these sorceries into high levels of sophistication in our modern times. This is seen in all forms of occultism and spiritism. We find them manifest in almost if not all religions, spiritual cults, spiritual movements etc. Today, it is even being used by some so called 'prophets' in Christendom.

Thus by being involved in all forms of unrighteousness, idolatry and sorcery and in practices with a similitude of the same, all the inhabitants of the earth, except for the elect few have been found to be influenced fully and saddled by the whore. To this end, they are considered to have committed fornication with her and were referred to as harlots. These were the same ones recorded in the scriptures as having worshipped the whore's beast and bearing his mark. Through the activities of the whore, the dragon is being worshipped by many. His ultimate aim is to own the soul of many and to be worshipped as God. There is yet another abomination mentioned in scriptures[11], which is not directly covered by the two discussed under the first vice of the whore. This however comes under the whore's second vice as the initiator and sustainer of the world systems and commerce.

6.3 THE WHORE AS THE MOTHER, INITIATOR, SOURCE AND SUSTAINER OF THE WORLD SYSTEM AND COMMERCE

This singular attribute of the whore is one of the most deceitful and deadly device she has employed in all her existence to accomplish the purpose of her being. We should bear in mind that the purpose of the whore's existence is:

1. To exalt the dragon's kingdom over and above the kingdom of God.

2. To oppose, hinder, or stop the worship of the Almighty God.

3. To replace the position of God in His congregation and temple[12]

In this course, she intends to get all the inhabitants of the earth to be her subjects. The whore being fully aware of this essence set out a double pronged strategy to accomplish this task. Her first strategy (or vice) has been discussed. In it we saw how she used that vice to successfully oppose, hinder, stop, and replace the worship due to God with the worship of the dragon, among the inhabitants of the earth. Over the years, from the foundation of the world, this has been her working principle. She devised another system alongside the first, capable of catching into her net every other inhabitant of the earth missed out by her first vice. This strategy is tagged the **WORLD'S SYSTEM**. It is one of the whore's most cunning and crafty device meant to assuredly accomplish the essence of her being.

Let us look at the different uses of the word **'WORLD'**: as identified in scripture and defined by the *Oxford Advanced Learner's Dictionary*.

WORLD: Relating to the earth, its nations, and people. This was used in 2 Peter 3:6 "whereby the world that then was, being overflowed with water perished". Some other examples are seen in John 14:13; 16:28; 17:5, 9, 11,13,15,18 and 21.

WORLD: Relating to a time, state, or scene of existence. For instance, when used in "this world and the next", and life on earth and existence after death. Some other scriptural examples are seen in Luke 20:34-35 and Matthew 12:32

WORLD: Relating to the material things and occupations of life (contrasted with the spiritual), the flesh, the mind, human affairs, societal opinions, customs, pleasures, etc.

This third usage of the word *world* is the one of interest to us. It is this world–made up of its commerce and systems–which the scriptures describe as "initiated and sustained by the whore". This is the very world referred to in the following scriptures:

John 14:30: "...for the prince of this world cometh, and hath nothing in me".

John 15:19: "if ye were of the world, the world would love his own; but because ye are not of the world, but I have chosen you out of the world, therefore the world hateth you".

6.0 Introducing the Great Whore (Mystery Babylon)

Matthew 16:26: "for what is a man profited if he shall gain the world, and lose his own soul?"

1 John 2:15-16: "Love not the world, neither the things that are in the world. If a man loves the world, the love of the Father is not in him. For all that is in the world, the lust (strong desires) of the flesh, and the lust of the eyes, and the pride of life is not of the Father but is of the world".

1 John 4:5: "They are of the world: therefore speak they of the world, and the world heareth them.

Right from the fall of Adam, the whore took over all the inhabitants of the earth (with only a few exceptions), turning the hearts of men away from God with her double pronged strategy. Note that from the fall of man, when man officially handed the kingdoms of the world given him by God to the dragon, and from the pronouncement of God thereafter[13], man came under the tribulation, terror or wrath of the dragon's kingdom (the whore). From that point, the whore ensured that man's essence for living will only center around (or that he will be preoccupied solely with) cares for food, clothing and shelter without paying any reasonable attention to God.

Under this second strategy (vice), she began to design and introduce the macro and micro economic policies of the whole world and the world governance systems. Using the seven-headed beast and his false prophet she designed the world's marketing policies and ideologies, introduced man's heavy laden work-hours and taxation systems, the use of money as a means of exchange, the international cross border trade liberalization policies, etc. Her activities did not stop at the development and modernization of the world commerce and systems; she further focused attention on developing extra-curricular activities that will give man pleasure and a tint of relief from all the tribulations she will cause man in his need for food, clothing and shelter[14]. These activities include prostitution, circuses, festivities, parties, sensual indulgence, sports, various forms of entertainment using audio-visual devices and the internet, etc.

The current world systems were designed and are currently sustained by the whore. It is all geared from the beginning, to make men care for nothing else but to 'feed the beast' by focusing their attention after the pursuit of food, clothing, shelter and pleasure without paying any reasonable attention to God. Thus, the music she is playing in all the civilizations of the world is materialism, acquisitions and status enhancement. Much as these things in themselves may not appear to be yokes of sin, she has a hidden agenda for developing them and that is, to turn men's affections, thoughts, desires, yearnings and attention away from God to the mundane things of this life, which are under her control. ***These pursuits are tantamount to covetousness and worldliness.*** There is a strong beguiling power in the use of the things of this world. The more we get the more we want to acquire. It is an insatiable desire in man which the prince of this world latches unto to cause men to pursue after the things of this world as if that is all there is to life. The consequence is that men become unfaithful in the use of the mammon of unrighteousness. All these pursuits and acquisitions, which are highly esteemed among men is another abomination[15] introduced by the whore which she has unfortunately caused many to partake in. It is the whore's most daring and seductive device of all ages. We will go ahead to correlate these things we have said here about the whore with the things written about her in Revelation 18.

From Rev.18:11-15 we see how the whore uses the commerce of the world covered by the merchandise of all that were written therein, which thrive under the luxuriant provisions and systems set out by her, to bring all the inhabitants of the earth under her. This world system and commerce is sustained by the life of the whore such that once she is judged and destroyed, they immediately collapse[16].

There is no activity on earth that involves payment for goods or services offered (i.e buying and selling) that does not come under the canopy of this world wide merchandise referred to in Revelation 18:11-15. If they are managers, accountants, or engineers working in the oil field, they are working to market oil from which they are paid. They are all together 'merchants of oil.' If they are car, airplane, or electrical parts manufacturers, they are identified as 'merchants of all varieties of objects of iron and the like.' They also come under the 'merchants of horses and chariots' as a means of transport and warfare. If they are workers in the cosmetics industries, they are considered as 'merchants of all sorts of ointments and perfume.' If they are farmers, they are identified as 'merchants of cereal and livestock.' If they are in the garment industry, they are 'merchants of all forms of apparel, inclusive of silk and scarlet.' If they are in the building or art industry, they are 'merchants of all forms of marbles and the like.' If you think of the finance and admin sector, they will be out of business if this world commerce is not in place. These come under the 'merchants of slaves and souls of men' (i.e *merchandise of services)*. The same goes for all the service sectors: hair salons, cafeteria, photography, rental services, medical, name it! No matter the profession or occupation, they are *'merchants of the earth'*[17], and the whole world commerce revolves around the contents of Rev.18:11-15 and is designed and sustained by the whore.

We can now conclusively see that our legitimate pursuit for food, clothing, shelter, (and pleasure to reduce the stress and the burden of our tribulation), could cause us to possibly partake of the life stream of the whore's wine, for all these things have their being in her. By partaking, we may be identifying ourselves with her and become intoxicated with the wine of her corruption and delicacies. Thus, whether you are working as an accountant, secretary, physician or personal assistant, farmer, director, manager, poor or rich, small or great, free or bond, marrying or giving in marriage, married or unmarried, partying, playing music, watching TV etc., we face the danger of being ignorantly swallowed up in this system not knowing and understanding the purpose of its initiator–the whore (Mystery Babylon). In this respect, her purpose is:

to captivate men with the mundane activities of the things of this life that they may not be able to pay any reasonable or fruitful attention to God and His kingdom.

By this means, she intends to succeed at enthroning her supremacy in the hearts of men and even over many of the elect of God, engraving the mark of her ownership (i.e. the mark of the beast) over them. The result of her success in this bid is that today, according to her design, men are more captivated by their careers and job than they are about God. Constrained by this world system they spend a great part of their lifetime outside their sleeping hours on the pursuit and development of their jobs and careers. Their remaining leisure time is spent on some of the earlier mentioned pleasure ridden activities; which is the stimulus of the entertainment industry. In this respect the whore reigns (sits) over multitudes, peoples, tongues and nations.

The whore can do absolutely nothing by herself; rather all her vices and attributes were directly expressed and enforced via the seven–headed beast that carried her and the false prophet which ministers before the beast. For this reason, the name of the whore's essence which is ***blasphemy*** was boldly written on each of the seven heads of the beast. According to the *Advance Learners Dictionary*, blasphemy in our context refers to everything that is offensive against God–***irreverence, sacrilegious, iniquity and resistance to God***. Consequently, the kingdom of God (*the Spirit of God's reign of righteousness in man*) has suffered violence and resistance right from the Garden of Eden. And the reverence due unto God has since then been contested by the dragon. This is blasphemy at work! Only in very few–the elect–has this reverence due unto God been preserved.

Thus from the beginning of the world to the second coming of Christ, from the beast of the Babylonian Empire to the beast of the Roman Empire, we find the dragon using the arm of the world governments, the unbelievers of all ages, all the fallen angels and all the tools at the disposal of his kingdom to enforce his vice;

- *To set up, propagate, nourish and ensure devotion to sin, idolatry and sorcery in place of devotion to the Almighty God among all the inhabitants of the earth.*
- *To set up, propagate and nourish the commerce and systems of the world and to ensure a world system where the children of men devote themselves to this system more than they do to the kingdom of God, so that the kingdom of God may be fruitless on earth.*

Most of the rich men and kings of the earth were ruled by the whore and were epitomes of power, affluence and worldliness. They were involved in and were used by the whore to encourage and to enforce the practice of all manner of sins, idolatry, sorcery, covetousness and worldliness. As a result, all the inhabitants of the earth joined them (as their leading models) to emulate and pursue after all manner of abominations: sins, sorcery, affluence, pleasure, materialism, etc. To constrain all flesh to this ungodly way of life, the seven-headed beast working through all the kings of the earth put in place ordinances and a world system resistant to godliness in which daily, men are constrained to work tirelessly for food, clothing and shelter; setting their affections, desires yearnings and imaginations on carnal things. These have had a deteriorative influence on the elect; wearing and making them overcharged with the cares and necessities of the things of this life.

This is the whole essence of the blasphemy against God. *It is this all-time great resistance against all godliness that entirely constitutes the event of the Great Tribulation.* To this end, from the on-set, Adam fell! The dragon set forth his deceitful devices, fought against this first-man-saint and overcame him. Since then, this great resistance or war against all godliness (and against the saints), has continued to rage. The dragon however, meets stiff contention with those few undaunted saints, who refuse to see their God blasphemed in their lives. But as far as he is concerned, everything in this world system designed by him must resist godliness. Therefore, the dragon's beast attacks these saints from all angles. He sends resistant government policies, extortionists, hunger, thirst, nakedness, distress, perilous times and death against them. If these would not succeed in weakening and diverting their attention from Christ to worldly things, then he sends deceivers among them to subvert them. These come under the very resemblance of Christ to ultimately deceive and confuse many, to the end that they may become more mindful of the cares and necessities of the things of this life than of the heavenly city to which they belong. By these, and many other fiery darts, the dragon succeeds at deflecting many from the truth causing their love for Christ to wax cold. ***This is the mystery of iniquity at work and blasphemy in action!*** God's desire is that we will face and contend with all these and yet be victorious hence it is written that those who do know their God shall be strong and do exploits. This strength is demonstrated through dissociating ourselves from the world system and refusing the lure of sin, sorcery, idolatry and love for pleasure, worldliness, wealth and materialism. We should bear witness to the fact that we are strangers and pilgrims on earth, looking for a city whose foundation and builder is God[18]. These are the kind of saints that will be dressed in white and come out of the Great Tribulation victorious.

Daniel's revelations show that the fourth beast, which is the seventh head and last kingdom in John's Revelation to bear rule over the earth, identified as the Roman Empire, will be more dreadful, terrible, and diverse and will do exceedingly more than those before it; devouring, breaking in pieces and stampeding the residue with the feet[19]. Much as the dragon will use the first six heads to enforce sin, idolatry and the world system upon all the inhabitants of the earth, the measure of his overwhelming influence and victory over many through the last head (Roman Empire) will be more devastating than all the others.

History has it that the Roman Empire "provided all of **Western civilization** and in fact, the entire world with an enduring and unrivaled socio-political, economic and cultural legacy"[20]. In the perspective of the Public Broadcasting Service, USA; the Roman Empire provided the tone for the civilizations of future generations which is still relevant today 2000 years later! Thus, it is on this foundation provided by the Roman Empire that the present world system and its commerce are based. The impact of the western civilization on all churches of the nations is the effective *worldlinization* of the saints. We have been subverted, polluted, disorganized, overthrown, trampled upon and swallowed up by this beast. For this reason, the scripture records that the seven–headed beast will use this world system to devastate Christendom (the seed of the woman who keep the testimony of our Lord Jesus Christ [21]). As a result, it is written that after he would have accomplished to scatter the power of the holy people, then shall Christ come to establish His kingdom on earth[22].

Today, the influence and triumph of this beast sitting over and trampling upon the church (the temple of God) is so alarming. The beast has effectively used this western civilization to make all the inhabitants of the earth (including the saints) to be so worldly minded. No wonder today the church has become so carnally (worldly) minded and saltless. Many of us have therefore followed after the societal legacies of this world and become so self-centered and self-seeking. Our yearnings and aspirations are more after the secular things of this life than after being like Christ in thought, word and deed. Just like the children of Israel, we have become so worn out, subverted and polluted. Hardly would you notice any difference between us and unbelievers. Our pride (feeling of satisfaction) is in material acquisitions. Churches are founded on the basis of profit, dissensions, schisms and rifts. We have all become so material (prosperity) conscious, much more than we seek after heavenly treasures. No wonder Jesus said that "...the children of this world have become wiser than the children of God's kingdom..." For the children of this world know how to pursue with an undivided loyalty, after all these things of the world and to get them; but the children of God's kingdom do not know how to pursue godliness without distraction and to possess it. Those things which are highly esteemed among the children of this world have unfortunately also become highly esteemed among us; regardless of the fact that these pursuits are abominations to the Lord[11]. Many present day Christians have become like Balaam–ready to do anything in a bid to acquire wealth or make a living. Most of us have lost focus of our course of being; we are scattered, disjointed and confused. As a compromise, we equate spirituality to the number of Christian programs and activities we are involved in which do not have much to contribute to our spiritual growth and character transformation. We claim to be dead and that the life we now live is Christ living it through us; but the truth is that the world and *self* are still alive in us, and Christ is obscured. He is not seen!

Thus the whore sits relaxed glorifying herself and operating comfortably, believing that she sits as a queen, and is not a widow and will not know any sorrow or loss of children[23]. This is because even after some of her children seem to have gained their freedom from her corruption and turn after righteousness, she still uses this world system to win them back to herself **unnoticed**. For this reason the voice went forth from heaven "come out of her my people..."[24]

6.0 Introducing the Great Whore (Mystery Babylon)

In this chapter, we have seen how the dragon used the seven-headed beast and all the members of his kingdom to resist the worship of God on earth. "Who can fight or withstand him–the children of men asked[25]. They were all so helpless under his yoke and influence; overtaken and following after all his ordinances and decrees, which were anti-Christ. He practiced and prospered in his intentions and devices. The record of the scripture at the conclusion of Revelation 13:8, concerning the seven-headed beast is that "all that dwell upon the earth shall follow after and worship him" with the exception of the elect. Unfortunately today, a host of us have stooped down and drunk from this cup of the wine of the abominations of Mystery Babylon; by pursuing after all these vain things. Many of us have become intoxicated with this whole corrupt system of the world. We have fallen in love with the world and have become her citizens rather than aliens and Pilgrims. This is the reason behind the present decay and worldliness in the churches. In chapter seven of this book, we will see in details, how the whore has used this world system to derail many from the faith. We should critically examine our lives to determine the vices of our enemy that has gained a foothold on us. We should then wash ourselves in the blood and put on the whole armor of God against the fiery darts of sin and deceit from the enemy.

May the Lord grant by the working of His Holy Spirit that we learn more of the Great Tribulation beyond what has been portrayed in these records from greater study of the scriptures. It is necessary for us to see all the issues from God's view point that we may not be deceived anymore by the whore. We will now proceed to correlate and bring down to our daily reality, this warfare.

END NOTES

1. Rev.14:8; Rev.17-18
2. Dan.7:1-7
3. Rev.14:8; 17:2; 18:3
4. Rev.17:5
5. Rev.18:11-17
6. Deut.7:25, 2 kings 23:5,13
7. 2 Kings23:13
8. Acts 19:35
9. Zeph.1:5
10. Gen.6:5, 8:21
11. see Luke 16:15

12. Isa.14:3; 2 Thes.2:4
13. Gen.3:17
14. Rev.18:22-23
15. Lk.16:15
16. Rev.18:10-11
17. Rev.18:11
18. Rev.7:9,13-14, Heb. 11:10-11
19. Dan.7:7
20. *American Encyclopedia vol.23 pg.686*
21. Rev.12:17; Rev.13:7
22. Dan.12:7
23. Rev.18:7; Isa 47:8
24. Rev.18:4,
25. Rev.13:4

Section 'C' – Application

Chapter Seven

7.0 The Nature of the Great Tribulation

From earlier referred accounts in the scriptures, we realized that the things that characterize the Great Tribulation include all natural and man-made disasters such as wars, pestilence, hunger/famine, earthquakes, oil gluts, flood, ravaging fires, unpredictable holocausts, depletion of the ozone layer, increasing sea level, global rise in inflation, terrorism etc. Also included are all the events of this life that cause great pain, trouble and sorrow such as: harsh economic policies, debt burdens, uncontrollable increase in crime rate, iniquity, idolatry, sexual immorality and lasciviousness etc[1]. All these work together to resist and impact on man's attention and worship of God.

7.1 CONTEMPORARY APPLICATION AND IMPACT ON THE CHURCH

Consistent with our analysis of the use and implication of the word ***Tribulation*** in Chapter 3 of this book; the account of Genesis 3:17 makes it clear that in man's bid to survive (feed, clothe and shelter himself), he will certainly face severe sorrows (tribulations). The account in Job 5:7 makes it clear that, man is born unto trouble (tribulations). As for the Preacher[2], all the travails a man has to go through in life for food, clothing and shelter are grievous and all his days are full of sorrows (tribulations). From Christ we learnt that as long as we are in this present world system, we will face tribulations[3]. And from Paul we learnt that we must go through much (great) tribulation to enter the kingdom of God[4]. These tribulations (sorrows) have been on the increase, starting from when man fell from the garden of Eden and the intensity will continue to increase until the second coming of Christ when God will wipe away the effect of these sorrows from the face of the victorious saints. These sorrows are the consequence of the dragon's presence on earth after being cast down to the earth and consequential to man's handing over of the world's kingdoms to the dragon. As long as this world system remains under the dragon's rule, he will torture, torment and trouble men with all these artfully crafted resistance. Furthermore, the dragon has also set diverse systems that will continually be stumbling blocks to man's bid to be reconciled to God. Having separated man from God and God's power, he provided an alternative in idolatry and all forms of sorceries, getting many yoked by compromise and particularly by coercion and sometimes by force.

The question that now comes to mind is: what is the essence of all these tribulations? The intention of the dragon is to ultimately and summarily retain man under his captivity and government. In the account of Paul in Romans 8:18-39 he made it clear that we have been called to be conformed to the image of Jesus Christ. But at the moment, all of us (including all creation and saints), groan in pain under the daily grievous resistance caused by the dragon. He went further and clearly marked out the purpose of these tribulations in Rom.8:35, saying "who shall separate us from the love of Christ? What shall ever be able to stop us or successfully resist us from triumphing over the dragon and being conformed to Christ and to His love? Then, he started enumerating some of the aforementioned devices of the whore that characterize the Great Tribulation. He asked, "Is it devastating trials and tribulations, or distress or persecution or famine (hunger, lack) or nakedness (lack of clothing and shelter) or peril (disease, perilous times) or sword (war) or death? Shall these things he asked, be able to swallow our affection (love), blur our vision or dampen our zeal, determination and yearning to be conformed to Christ? *Such questions asked by Paul gives a clear picture of the purpose or essence of these tribulations; to swallow up our love for Christ, to the end that we may not become conformed to Christ or be glorified to reign with him.*

In Christendom, all the aforementioned devices of the dragon that characterizes the Great Tribulation which Paul was persuaded will not dampen

our love; have unfortunately today made the love of many for Christ to wax cold. When you consider the effect of open and free expressions of immorality, nudity, lasciviousness, terrorism, armed robbery and love for pleasure and quest for wealth, mass communicated via the print and audio visual media to the entire human race; then you will understand how these have effectively dampened and eroded our love and concentration on Christ. What of the ever increasing bills, job loss due to ailing economies or even the heat of the sun and consequent rat race that have driven us sore and far away from the love of Christ, in our pursuit of success? These are just a few. The target remains the same; *to sap our spiritual strength and frustrate our personal devotion to the calling of God upon us.*

From our studies, we can safely infer that the mundane activities of the things of this life, which are all directly under the prince of this world, are divergent to the things of God. Unbelievers enthusiastically pursue after these things and therefore come under the mark (or influence) of the beast. The challenge the prince of this world has in this respect is with the believers. But he has also won some landslide victory in this respect. For this reason, the whore sits luxuriantly saying she is not a widow and will not lose her children[5], because even after getting born again, she has succeeded in enticing us after the same pursuits of all these mundane things of this life (food, clothing, shelter, prosperity, success, etc.) at the expense of our calling, attempting to and in most cases succeeding at bringing us back under her influence.

The need to fend for oneself for food, clothing and shelter is not a sin but the pursuit after the cares and necessities of this life as if that is the essence of your being and at the expense of your personal devotion to Christ, is what is not right before the Lord. As we have learnt so far, the mystery of iniquity behind them is that; they are designed and set to distract us from giving necessary and overwhelming attention to Christ. Without an all-consuming affection and attention on Christ, the believer can hardly bear the heavenly fruits that would stand the test of time. All these engrossing affection after the things of this world is what Jesus referred to as the 'abundance of iniquity' that will make the love of many toward Him to wax cold.

The mystery behind the abundance of iniquity is what the beast has today successfully used in making believers so worldly minded, filled with activities from the beginning to the end of each day. We are consumed, overtaken, absorbed and devoted to the cares and necessities of the things of this life, with only very little attention to Christ. Therefore, our lives portray us in a form of 'worldly successes' in place of 'Christ likeness'; worldliness in place of godliness; mark of the beast in place of the mark of Christ. The same significant amount of time, energy and attention required to achieve 'worldly successes', is the same that is required to make a mark at being like Jesus. Our enemy has succeeded in coining the world system in such a way that it seems difficult for any man to give this expected devotion to the need of being conformed to Christ, and at the same time, be able to meet up with the needs and responsibilities of this life. *Christ, aware of this fact, told us not to be afraid or set our hearts after these things, but after heavenly things;* ***for He will undertake to care for us.*** But the fear and threats of accumulating bills however, keep driving us sore after these things. Also, the silent tormenting yearning for an improved social status puts so much pressure on us and succeeds in stirring our affections after an insatiable quest for worldly treasures.

The world is moving so fast that we are afraid to slow down lest we lose out in our expected pursuits and acquisitions. Constrained by this world system, we work tirelessly from morning till evening for food, clothing, shelter (and pleasure) and we only come home in the evenings tired and exhausted, unable to even give Christ any reasonable attention. We end up retiring to our pleasure-ridden activities to pacify/placate the stress and tribulations of the day. What do we think made Jesus to say that "sufficient unto the day is the evil thereof"? Is it not because, all the things that distract us daily from His presence (our work, thoughts, pleasures, etc.) are enough evil in themselves? And we should not compound these evil (distractions) by taking thought about the ones that would come with the next day.

This circumstance unfortunately has affected many of our full time ministers of the gospel, who though called to attend solely unto Christ, today, indulge themselves in the management of the churches and so many church and secular activities at the expense of their personal devotion to the Lord. Thus we do not find them wholesomely exemplifying Christ; rather some of them have ended up becoming vehicles by which the whore deceives many. Many of them are now after the pleasures of the things of this life, as the unbelievers are, unfortunately using the course of the gospel as a means of gain. There are however, a few who truly have given themselves devotedly to the person of Christ or in other words, pursuit of His presence. As for the rest, they are all drunk with the desires, yearnings and pursuit after the things of this world and have lost sight of the knowledge of the Lord. Their hearts are more set after building up their cathedrals, ministries and possessions than they are set at the feet of Jesus. Without realizing it, they are serving under the whore as vehicles of our present confusion, segregation and worldliness in the church. This was the same kind of backsliding the Lord discovered among the Israelites that He gave them a 'bill of divorce'. Most of them from the least to the greatest were so given to covetousness. Their prophets and priests dealt falsely; saying 'peace' (amidst all their backsliding, telling them that all was well), when there was no peace. [6] They made the people err and taught and prophesied for a fee[7]. We were supposed to have learnt from their mistakes and pitfalls. Unfortunately, we have become so much in love with our present world, delighting in almost any new thing our eyes behold. Yearning, pursuing, acquiring and never getting satisfied. These same things do the people of the world go after and there's been little or no difference between us and them. Therefore in loving the world, we have associated ourselves with mystery Babylon and have become drunk with the wine of worldliness.

In the bid of being spiritual, the enemy has made most of us now mistake involvement in multiplicity of church activities as a measure of spirituality. We should realize that the only reasonable service required of us from the Lord is the continual presentation of our selves at His feet for the purpose of being transformed by the renewing of our mind into His personality[8]. It is good to be involved in the work of the kingdom no doubt but in our service the quality of our lives should show the transforming power of Christ.

From another perspective and to cushion the effect of the incessant stressful world system on the saints, we have heaped up for ourselves ministers of 'miracles and prosperity' and have pressured and compelled other faithful ministers into focusing their ministerial efforts on miracles and prosperity only. These have now become our yard stick for assessing success in Ministry. Any minister, ministry or church in which these are not manifest daily, is considered 'not happening' and is not well recognized in Christendom! We do not undermine the value of miracles and prosperity in building up the body, for they are part of the package of our salvation. However, unbalanced teachings that turns the attention of Christians toward these things and making them our priorities has rather led many into satan's trap. Through it, the enemy has effectively distracted the saints from the essence of their calling. ***All we have been given to as a result of all these prosperity teachings is COVETOUSNESS–pursuit of worldly treasures. It is also the bedrock of the doctrine of Balaam.*** This was the case in Lk.12:1-14 where Christ was eager about passing heavenly treasures (the knowledge of the Father) across to the multitude, but a recipient in the crowd was rather more mindful about 'bread' –food, clothing and shelter. Jesus, upset by this stance retorted, *"who made me a judge or divider* *over you...beware of covetousness, for a man's life does not consist of the abundance (or otherwise) of the things he possesses. We seem not to understand or remember that it is easier for God to make a camel pass through the eye of a needle than it is for Him to make a man given to all these pursuits to enter into His kingdom.*

Can we now understand better how the beast has so coined our world system in such a way that it is so difficult for anyone to buy or sell without taking his mark? Both the poor and rich, small and great, free and bond has been caught in this web. **Brethren, this mystery of iniquity is at work causing the love of many of us to wax cold. You can either set your love on the kingdom of Christ or set it on the kingdom of the dragon. The two don't go together. They are two different worlds with opposing marks of identification!**

We earlier described the beast's intention for establishing this worldwide 'buying and selling' or *'merchandization'* system; such that all men on earth might be brought under his mark. Money is the means and major essence of transaction in this buying and selling. In our legitimate pursuit of money, we may be found to be more attached and given to this pursuit than we are given to pursuing after Christ. This is the root of **all evil** on earth and a major underlying factor behind the present worldliness in the churches. Due to negligence of this truth, many of us who started in the Spirit are now ending up in the flesh!

All the members of the whore relentlessly go to and fro in the whole world seeking to destroy, resist, trample and scatter the power of the holy people and to withstand every one that calls on the name of God. She uses her visible members–the unbelievers–to lynch and stifle our undivided loyalty and attention to Christ. They challenge and entice us by their seeming success and sophistication, making us appear like non-performers and failures. As a result, we are stirred and lured after these same pursuits for wealth, pleasure and the material things of this life which make us feel successful according to the standards set by the world. In one instance, the lady that is married to a poor husband or barren or unmarried at an advanced age is made to feel that her world is a tragedy. As a result she gets encumbered, engrossed, mindful and broody over this need and care. On the other hand, the man who has not been able to raise enough possessions from his career, made a name among the successful and rich is made to feel that he is a failure and a non-performer. As a result, he gets stirred after every available means to become successful. These pursuits, yearnings and cravings to be like the people of the world around us, end up making us so worldly minded and eroding all the godliness there is among the brethren. ***This is how the dragon succeeds in scattering the power of the holy people. And this in effect is the falling away of the saints from the truth, which has been prophesied long ago concerning our age***[9].

We therefore recognize that one major subtle way through which the whore executes her resistance against the saints is by attracting their affection and attention away from God through the luster of these things. For this reason Jesus warned us to beware lest we become captivated and overcharged by the cares and necessities of the things of this life and that day takes us unawares[10]. The combined effect of all the aforementioned devices of the whore is the gradual but effective eroding and wearing out of our love for Christ. We also discovered that the major channel through which either God or the dragon reigns over a man is through the man's mind. By the things which a man sets his mind on, the spirit directly in charge of those things gradually gains control over the heart of such a man. For this reason, the scripture enjoined us to set our affections (mind, imaginations) on things above, seeking the treasured qualities and knowledge of our Lord Jesus Christ[11]. The dragon himself does not want to see us bear these fruits (qualities of Christ or mark of Christ or treasures of heaven). To this end, he uses all manner of things under his disposal to resist us.

On one hand, he applies pressure on our minds through increasing bills (school fees, rents, food, car and sundry expenses), inflation, accidents, armed robbery, death of a bread winner, etc. On another hand, he uses open and free expressions of immorality, lasciviousness, love for pleasure and quest for wealth, which he also mass communicates via the print and electronic media upon the entire human race, to defray our attention or minds from Christ. As a result of all these fiery darts of our enemy coming upon us from all angles, our focus on Christ (or seeking after heavenly things) wanes and our love, devotion, yearning and zeal after Christ waxes cold. It is for this reason that the Spirit of Christ in us is envious[12]; for we have given our minds and hearts more to the things of this world than we have given to Him[13].

Another weapon the enemy has been using is the introduction of 'error and confusion' regarding milestones in God's calendar. It has thrived because of ignorance and lack of knowledge. Our enemy–the anti-Christ–has made us believe that he is yet to come. Unknown to us, he has been working under cover, causing so much havoc and wrecking the whole of Christendom–***this is Mystery at work. He has coined the world in such a way that we hardly have the time to study the scriptures and for lack of this knowledge we perish.***

Meanwhile Jesus made it clear in Jn.17:3 that the eternal life the Father instructed Him to give to us is the very knowledge of God and Christ. But how can we know Him when we don't have time to study and be taught by His Spirit? For this reason we are frail and feeble and cannot withstand the fiery darts of the enemy. It is painful to see this happening, even though it has been prophesied that after he would have accomplished to scatter the power of the children of God, then shall the end come[14]. Our God however said, that those He loves, He corrects and chastises. For this reason He is calling us to the knowledge of this truth and to take the next step of action which is to come out of her (Mystery Babylon).

The good news is that God will never leave his children without a way out, especially in overcoming their enemy. To ensure we prepare to meet the bridegroom, we must wear our wedding garment. To help us understand how to do this, we will now take a look at "the Essence of Our Being" and "the Pathway to Follow".

7.2 THE ESSENCE OF OUR BEING

The intention for which God called all of us after Christ, is to be made to conform to Christ. *To be born again is not an end in itself, but a means to an end. The essence is to be groomed, trained, transformed and adopted to become exactly like Jesus of Nazareth.* This was what Jesus had in mind when He said it has become absolutely necessary for a seed to die so that it can **bring forth** many other seeds with exactly the same genetic characteristics as the original seed. The act of being 'made' to conform to the image of Jesus is a process which is directly dependent on the measure to which a man gives himself to that essence. Remember that God has made available everything we need for this race and all we need to bring forth 'fruit'. If it were not so, the parable of the sower will be irrelevant to us. We need to culture the word that has been planted in our heart, jealously de-stoning our hearts, plucking out all tares and watering it, to ensure it brings forth fruits. Thus, when a man is solely given to this essence, he attains this conformation by faith and is clothed with the wedding gown. Unless a man is made to conform to this image, he is not glorified. Eph. 4: 20 -24 clearly instructs us to ensure that the 'old man' in us dies and in its place we should put on the garment of the 'new man' which is renewed by the Spirit of God after righteousness.

7.0 The Nature of the Great Tribulation

Some of us may argue at this point that it is by grace that we are saved or justified through faith and not by works, lest any man should boast[15]. ***Yes, it is true; but faith also has its works or else it is dead*** [16]. It is solely of God that we are called. But as for our entering His kingdom; a great deal of commitment on our part is required to that end. We are the ones to work out our salvation in fear and trembling following the counsel of His Holy Spirit to ensure we do not falter or come short of the promise to enter into His rest; for not all who are called, shall be chosen. Our mind must be renewed for our lives to be transformed. The chosen are those who dissociate themselves from this present iniquity which is at work, which Christ prophesied will make the love of many to wax cold. In its place, they dedicated themselves to the essence of their creation (which is to be conformed to Christ) and they follow the Lamb of God wherever He goes[17].

God cannot be deceived. He knows those whose hearts are truly set after Him; those whose affections, yearnings and love are glued on Him, to be conformed to Christ. These ones are they that detest and abhor the mundane things of this world and in its place violently pursue after Christ. This is not about the outward show of wearing a long, sad and depressed face, a particular mode of dressing, cursing unbelievers or refusal to watch TV, use facial make-ups etc. It is an inward character transformation by the Spirit that brings forth a man beyond reproach. Such saints live and yet not them but Christ lives in them. Their whole being is focused on Him that they might by beholding Him as in a mirror be transformed from one level of glory to another unto the very image of Christ. These are the ones that have denied self to follow Christ. Even if they have lived on earth for only twenty-four hours, Christ knows these ones because they set their love on Him. They have put on the wedding robe waiting for His coming. They live in the consciousness of this world not being theirs, eagerly expecting the new world to which they belong. All their affections, thoughts, desires and imaginations are set on heaven and not on the things of this life. Romans 8:6 made it clear that these ones who are mindful after the heavenly treasures in Christ have life (or the wedding robe of Christ). But those who though born again, are still full of thoughts, affections and desires of the things of this life, may miss out of the kingdom of God[18]. We are called, chosen and designated to be Saints – *holy*[19]. Christ came to make an end of sins, to make reconciliation for iniquity, to bring in everlasting righteousness and to rededicate the holy habitation of God[20]. ***We are that habitation: called and set apart by faith through the grace of God to be holy habitation of God***[21]. We are His house of prayer and communion not a place of merchandize. Let us hold this forth!

7.3 THE PATHWAY TO FOLLOW (PUT ON YOUR WEDDING GARMENT)

Having seen that the whole world system; its merchandise and government, societal values and ideologies are all under the whore–**Mystery Babylon**– what kind of life or pathway to godliness should we follow in order to escape the dangers of this present darkness? The following pathways as identified by Christ provide answers to this quest.

- A. Where a man's heart is[22]
- B. Where a man's eye is[23]
- C. Loving either God or Mammon[24]
- D. Seeking after the things of this life or after the kingdom[25]
- E. The Process[26]
- F. The Place of the Holy Spirit

A. WHERE A MAN'S HEART IS (Matt.6:19-22)

Recognize here that a man can either lay treasures in heaven or on earth (i.e world). Whichever one is the case, where a man's treasures are; there he will fix his heart. It is critical to know where our hearts are fixed as this helps us know if we are heaven or hell bound. ***Remember as it is written that the heart of a man is above all things deceitful and desperately wicked***[27]. Men have been grossly deceived by their hearts. Even the believers, don't seem to have a very clear assessment of where their hearts are. Due to this ignorance, our hearts have deceived many of us, making us comfortable with all manner of the things of this world that are evil in the sight of God. In fact the scripture here invariably makes it clear that it is imperative to know, understand and control our hearts, otherwise it could present a much more deceptive and destructive device within us than our well known enemy that is outside. So how do we know where a man's heart is? (Or according to Jeremiah 17:9, who knows or understands the heart of man?)

7.0 The Nature of the Great Tribulation

The Lord God is the one that will help us search and try the reins of our heart to understand where our heart is[28]. The man of understanding in Proverbs 23:7 says that *"as a man thinketh in his heart, so is he"*. Therefore, to know the things happening in a man's heart or what he is made up of, or to know where his heart is: ***x-ray his thoughts***! The picture of his thought pattern (or what happens in his mind) gives you a clear vision of where his heart belongs and who he is.

In Robert Liardon's account of William Braham in his book *God's Generals*, an angel while discussing with William, also equated the knowledge of the very secret of men's heart to an understanding of men's thought. Thus, ***the mind is the mirror of the heart.*** And the very thoughts that go on in our minds are the very pictures that depict what we look like before God. Some extreme types of the evil thoughts that can captivate a man's thought include murder, adultery, fornication, theft, bearing false witness, etc. All that manifest such fruits (works) are they that bear the mark of the beast and shall not enter the kingdom of God[29]. We also observe that all through the day, men's hearts and thoughts are captivated after all the cares and necessities of this life. Unfortunately, these are the same things we clearly pointed out earlier as having been mapped out by the whore via the seven-headed beast and the false prophet to turn men's heart and attention away from God. Some of these things we had earlier pointed out may not be categorically evil in themselves, but the evil behind them is that they are designed to distract us from setting out thoughts after Christ and His nature (i.e heavenly treasures). To this end, a man's heart is enticed and affectionately disposed after all these cares leading to laying treasures on earth rather than in heaven.

Thus, we conclude that what goes on in our mind daily gives a clear picture of where our hearts are. *If your mind is set on the things of this life, then you will be laying treasures on earth. In other words, you **treasure** more the things of this life, therefore your thoughts are set on them and you pursue after them. But if your mind is set on the pursuit of Christ and heavenly things, then* you *will be laying treasures in heaven*. We can also see a man's heart through their words and works; for out of the abundance of the heart the mouth speaks and the body works. It is for this reason the Lord emphasized in the account of Jeremiah 17:9-10, that 'where a man's heart is set' can be known conclusively by the works or fruits he bears. Therefore, as soon as a man is found in his heart to be engulfed with the pursuit of the things of this life rather than after heavenly things, he is in respect to this perspective of God, identifying himself with the prince of this world and could as a result be bearing the mark of the beast. This pathway to life therefore calls for us to set our minds and thoughts at the feet of Jesus, continually beholding and craving after the treasured qualities, knowledge and values of our heavenly kingdom.

B. WHERE A MAN'S EYE IS (Matt.6:22-23)

The eye is the focal view point (or sight instrument) of the body. The inference here is that once this view or focal point is set on the light of the world (i.e Jesus Christ), the whole body shall be full of that light (i.e. qualities of Jesus Christ) and such a person is identified with the mark of Jesus Christ. But when it is set on all the mundane things of this life (including all our needs, wants, hardship, tribulations, lacks, sufferings, acquisitions, status quo, etc.), that person shall be eclipsed with darkness and identified with the mark of the beast. For this reason it is written: *"If ye then be risen with Christ seek those things which are above, where Christ sitteth on the right hand of God. Set your affection on things above, not on things on the earth*[30]. This same requirement is echoed in Romans 12:1-2; for once a man consistently focus, seek and present himself to the Lord, which is declared as his reasonable service, then and only then shall he be transformed into the likeness of our Saviour and King Jesus Christ. This is also what the scripture means when it says *"abide in Christ"* – **stay your mind on Him**. It is as we set our eyes and focus on Christ that the Holy Spirit will begin to develop the character of Christ in us. While beholding Him as in a mirror we are transformed into the very image of Him that we see[31]. It is a free gift that is not merited by our works, but comes as we set our eyes and love on Him seeking His presence, studying His word at His feet and listening to His Holy Spirit. It is only by this principle that we can attain unto the fullness of Christ and be able to sustain this nature or mark of Christ with the passing of time. I have not attained myself, but I yearn after this pressing towards the mark of the prize of the high calling of God in Christ Jesus[32].

C. LOVING EITHER GOD OR MAMMON (Mth.6:24)

Here, we see Jesus separating all men into two camps: by the things written in this verse, every man was 'marked' or 'identified' as either God's or the Mammon's. Thus every man can only

i. Serve either GOD or Mammon

ii. Hate (despise) either GOD or Mammon

iii. Love either GOD or Mammon

Some of us have narrowed down this 'mammon' to money or mere riches. *It is a much more embracing concept that is resistant to the kingdom of God.* It covers all the pursuits of man on earth for self-actualization. That is why it is compared as a direct opposite to 'true riches' or heavenly treasures in Luke 16:11. James supported this verse when he passionately asserted that friendship with this WORLD is enmity with God[33]. The word of difference used by James– 'friendship/enmity'– is the same as the 'love/hate' used in Matthew 6:24. In other words, mammon further represents the world systems and commerce. Except a man recognize and understand how to be faithful in the use of this mammon of unrighteousness the 'true riches' cannot be committed to him.

This scripture directs us to detest this world system we are in and in its place yearn, crave, and passionately fix our thoughts and desires on Christ. Otherwise we would find ourselves delighting in, pursuing, craving and attending unto all the cares and necessities of the things of this life at the expense of our pursuit after Christ. *They both don't agree and are in contention against each other. You will have to choose which camp to belong. By the fruits you bear (or your works), you will be showing forth the marks of him you bear-whether they are that of Christ or that of the beast.* This is also clearly depicted in the following scriptures:

> *Love not the world; neither the things that are in the world. If any man loves the world, the love of the father is not in him. For all that is in the world, the lust of the flesh, and the lust of eyes, and the pride of life, is not of the father, but is of the world* [34].

Applying the *Advance Learners Dictionary* interpretation of the words love and lust, we can render this verse as follows:

> *Do not **like, fancy, crave for, strongly desire, delight, relish, or set thoughts and imaginations** on this world or anything that is in this world. If you do that, you certainly do not love God, rather you are his enemy.*

For all that is in the world; **the strong desires for, and the passionate enjoyment of anything in this life (whether they be plum jobs, career, hobbies, games, parties, orgies, sophistication, wealth, etc);** *or the pride* **(feeling of satisfaction)** *of life, is not of the Father, but is of the world* [35].

D. SEEKING AFTER THE THINGS OF THIS LIFE OR AFTER THE THINGS OF THE KINGDOM OF GOD (Matt.6:25, 31-34)

In this verse (Matt.6:25), Jesus summarized the pathways signifying that they refer to the same things. The word 'therefore' is usually used in summarizing a fact someone must have been trying to pass across. This means that the statement "therefore take no thought for your life", summarily represents the fact Jesus has been trying to pass across in A, B and C above. This instruction brings to fore the fact that 'taking thought' is the premise for either laying treasures in heaven or on earth. By this Jesus equated it to loving either God or Mammon. It then implies that in 'taking thought' or 'seeking after' our lives (for food, clothing, shelter and pleasure) at the expense of our calling; or by setting our hearts and eyes after these things which all the Gentiles according to Matt.6:32 are also engaged in, we may be found to have cherished and delighted in the things of this world and not in Him. The Lord said He is aware of all our needs. Nevertheless, He made it clear from the foregoing that it is evil to be MIND-FULL of them; for so it is with the Gentiles. Unfortunately today, we have esteemed 'attending unto' and 'minding' all our cares and necessities far above the essence of our calling.

Can we now see the measure of the danger we are facing? Much as we are born again, we are living so close to spiritual death. Paul captured these thoughts in his epistle to the Romans when he said that, to be in Christ and yet 'walk after' (i.e be mindful of or seek after) all these things is death. For they that are carnal do set their minds on the things of the flesh (food, clothe, shelter and pleasure), but they that are of the Spirit set their minds on the things of the Spirit (heavenly mindedness). The carnally minded person is in enmity against God and cannot please Him[36]. Usually, we unconsciously feel that once we are born again it means we have first sought the kingdom of God and its righteousness, and that we can then seek after all our cares and necessities. As long as we are in this body however there should be no end to our seeking after the kingdom of God and its righteousness. To seek the kingdom of Christ means to seek the wholesome reign of the Spirit of Christ in us. When you stop focusing on Christ, you would no longer be able to bear fruit. This is the reason it is dangerous to think you know it all as a Christian or that 'you have arrived'. Do we really think we have arrived? If we have, then he that sees us should be seeing Jesus Christ. Therefore, each of us should have a willing and open heart to learn of the Lord, be accountable to Him and to one another and allow our feet to be washed by one another. The pathway calls for us not to relax in the warfront as this is dangerous. But we should patiently and diligently set our hearts on Christ, refusing all distractions from Him, until we see Him in us by His Spirit.

E. THE PROCESS (Matt.16:24-26)

Here Jesus categorically earmarks the conditions a man must first meet, if he wants to follow Him or bear His mark. He makes it clear that the person must: *first deny himself, take up his cross and follow him. Thus, until a man has been able to first and foremost, deny himself, he can by no means follow Christ. Though such a one calls on the name of the Lord, and may perform wonders in His name, the person cannot be transformed by Christ.* Such a one may be denied by Christ on the last day as one of those that believed they served him through numerous activities and miracles but, never really loving Him. A man's 'self' consist of his nature, special qualities, interests and pleasures. It is that part of a man that desires to be admired, actualized, glorified, satisfied and recognized.

The implication of what Jesus is saying here is that the man who wishes to follow this pathway, must first and foremost deny the interests and pleasures of the things of this life that his 'self' is already set on which distracts him from attending unto God. And in its place take up his cross (i.e vigorously pursue the essence of our being–which is to be conformed to the image of Christ– setting all his yearning, affections, desires, delight, fancy, ambition, craving (**love**), after Him (Jesus) to lay hold on this heavenly treasure. *Christ is saying that only when these conditions are met can a man come under His discipleship and truly be identified by him with His mark.* It is for this reason Paul instructed us saying; let this mind be in you which was also in Christ Jesus, counting as loss every other thing you have identified yourself in the world with before and in its place pursuing after the mark for the prize of the high calling of God in Christ Jesus[37].

Jesus in another account in Matt.11:28-30 offered to us His yoke and burden. *A yoke is a restrictive device used for bearing and carrying a burden.* This means that in 'taking His yoke upon us' and 'bearing His own burden' which is light, we will experience rest from our heavy burdens. ***His yoke refers to "come unto Me", and His burden refers to "learn of me".*** When a man breaks off the yoke and distress of the pursuit of his self and puts on Christ's yoke (***i.e restricts himself to the presence of Christ***) to bear His burden (***i.e learn of Him***) such a man will find an extra ordinary kind of relaxed mindset amidst all his needs and troubles. Though he works like every other man, the burden in his heart is *"Jesus please let me see Your face I want to be like You"*. His affections are glued on the things above and he delights not in the system of the world. In the midst of His work, he sees Jesus to whom he is yoked (i.e *to whom he has restricted his attention to)*, learning continually from Him. He sees not himself living for his own pleasure but Him that died for him and is now living in him. He willingly gives up every other thing that he has interest or pleasure in, which distracts him from attending unto the Lord, for the sake of knowing, learning and being at the feet of Jesus. Thus he finds dwelling in him an indescribable form of peace which the world cannot give. This is the peace that calms all our tribulations[38].

Part of what the lord has thought me as a way to go through the tribulations of our time and come out victorious is by not being **'mind-full'** of all my cares, needs, lacks and wants but in its place, be **'mind-full'** of this yearning to continually conform to the image of Jesus Christ. For the man who seeks to save (find or pursue after) his life shall lose it. But the man that will regard these cares and necessities as unimportant, refusing to be distracted by them for the excellence of attending unto and knowing Christ as Lord, will find his life. This is the basic principle that results in an effective self-denial. Based on this foundation the person now enters into a wonderful relationship with Christ in which he walks daily by every word proceeding from the mouth of Christ. He does not do anything of his own accord but that which Christ tells him. He is said to be dead and he is no longer the one living but Christ living through him. It is under this condition that Christ finds fulfillment in a man.

To the man therefore who wishes to tread this pathway of life, I encourage; restrict yourself continually to the presence of Christ meditating on His words at all times, whether you are working in a factory, hospital, school, no matter how noisy or seemingly distressful the job is or your environment may be. Be consistent in season and out of season in your resolve to attend continually unto the Lord learning at His feet. Attend unto Him amidst all your schedules, constantly focusing and seeing Him in all things, determining not to allow the systems and environment in which you work to turn your affection and attention away from your essence of living. By now you understand that the whore designed these systems and sits on them to use them in distracting you. As you rejoice and relish in His presence, continually having fellowship and learning of Him, then you shall find rest and the mark of Jesus solidly engraved on you. By this, you will not partake of the iniquities of the great whore (which in this case is to turn men's heart away from God, so that in their being distracted they will not be able to give Christ the room to groom and disciple them into being like himself).

F. THE PLACE OF THE HOLY SPIRIT

Before Jesus left earth, He handed us over to another person in His place that will be with us individually, walk with us, talk with us, share life's experiences together with us and teach us about our Father. Just as Jesus walked the face of the earth with His disciples, so this person will walk the face of the earth with us. Through the person of the Holy Spirit, Christ Himself and our Father will be fully expressed through us in this life. This person whom He called "the Comforter" is the same one, by whom Zerubabbel fulfilled and finished his course[39]. By Him also, Christ executed the course of the Father on earth[40]. By Him also if we choose, shall every one of us execute the course of God upon us. Thus, to be fully acquainted with Him and to know to walk and work with Him is paramount, if we must have any place in Christ. In fact living by every word that proceeds from His mouth daily, has been highlighted in scriptures as the mark that identifies the children of God[41].

It is by this Spirit of God that we shall be led into the fullness of Christ. For this reason as Christ was leaving, He directed us to the Holy Spirit instructing us to attend unto Him. Unfortunately today, He is only called upon at the times of our need, but the idea of living by every word that proceeds from Him has been relegated to the background. Jesus made it clear, that once we are acquainted with Him, He will teach us much more than all our teachers preserve and lead us into all truth and no one will be able to deceive us. But most of our ministers have unintentionally relegated the position of the Holy Spirit to the background preferring rather that we depend on them (the ministers) for every truth we shall learn. This is one of the reasons we are in so much spiritual mess in the churches today; confused and ignorant of the fact that our enemy is almost pulling the carpet from under our feet.

May God help us see and to retrace our steps back to the Holy Spirit. God once taught me that if the ministers can introduce the church (sheep) to the Holy Spirit, and get them to learn to walk/work with Him, they would have accomplished the major assignment required of them as ministers. When the Lord further taught me about the place of His seven foldSpirit in the life of every believer, I was so greatly fascinated that I asked Him, "Lord, why didn't You teach this same thing to your ministers? If You had done so Lord, they would have presented a better image of You than they have presently done". Then the Lord responded, "Are they willing to make the sacrifice?" Then I answered, "Lord, which sacrifice will be too much for us to make as long as it is to know You? The highest sacrifice You may ask of us is to withdraw into full time ministry and not to marry, which some of us are already doing." Then the Lord said, "That is only secondary." I went further, "Lord You mean that these things that are highly respected among us today as hallmarks of spirituality are only but secondary? What then is the primary sacrifice that we cannot pay?" Then the Lord answered, *"It remains that those that are married, be as though they were not married, those that buy and sell as though they possess nothing, and those that make use of this world's goods as not abusing them or allowing them abuse you, that you may all know to attend unto Me without distraction."*

Understanding this is key if we must overcome in this Great Tribulation. In other words, our present-engrossing pursuits for resources to take care of the ministry and family's feeding, shelter, pleasure and sundry bills have a subtle way of veering our thoughts, hearts and passions from Christ and setting them after this idolized luster of being successful. Therefore, we should not let our minds be captivated or absorbed by these cares, that we may know to rather set our minds, thoughts, desires and yearnings without distraction after the Lord. Furthermore, we should not feel elated or fulfilled by reason of what we own or have accomplished, neither should we be down cast because we lack any worldly goods; such are abuses. A full text on this was issued by the Holy Spirit through Paul in 1 Cor.7:25-32.

If we can walk in the light of this understanding, this book would have achieved its objective.

END NOTES

1. Matt.2:6-8, Rev.7:16, 21:24, Gen.3:17-19, Job 5:7, Ecc.2:22-23, Jn.16:33, 1Tim.4:1-2, 2 Tim 3:1-7, Acts 14:14-22
2. Eccl. 2: 22-23
3. Jn.16:33
4. Act 14:22
5. Is.47:8, Rev.18:7
6. Jer.3:8, 8:10-12
7. Micah 3:5,11
8. Rom.12:1-2
9. 2 Thes.2:3
10. Lk.21:34
11. Col.3:1-2
12. James 4:5
13. James 4:4
14. Dan.12:7
15. Rom.3:24
16. James 2:17
17. John 12:26, Rev.14:4
18. Rom.8:1, 5-8
19. Rom.1:7; 1Cor.1:2; Eph.1:4; Phil.1:1; Col.1:2
20. Dan.7:24, Heb.2:17
21. 1Cor.3:17
22. Matt.6:19-21
23. Matt.6:22-23
24. Matt.6:24
25. Matt.6:25, 31-34
26. Matt.16:24-27
27. Jer.17:9
28. Jer.17:10
29. Rev.21:8
30. Col.3:1-2
31. 2 Cor.3:18
32. Phil.3:14
33. James4:4
34. 1 John 2:15-16
35. 1 John 2:15-16, *paraphrased*
36. Rom.8:1-6

37. Phil.3:7-16 *paraphrased*
38. Jn.14:27
39. Zechariah 4:6-10
40. Isaiah 11:1-3; Rev.3:1
41. Rom 8:1, 14; Matt.4:4

Chapter Eight

8.0 Conclusion

This study focused on helping Christians understand the warfare we face as individuals and as a church, how it is playing out today and how we can activate the victory we have in Christ. It contains no new doctrine but simply the exposition of how a possible misunderstanding of the timing, key players and nature of the Great Tribulation may have been used by the enemy to further the agenda of kingdom of darkness.

Following these studies, we came to the conclusion that the **GREAT TRIBULATION** we were expecting in the future has been, presently is, and will continue till the end of times. Its intensity has been increasing and the resistance we are facing in this century has become fiercer than that which the saints faced all through the centuries past.

We want to acknowledge that in discussing this subject, we may have presented a view of the timing and nature of the Great Tribulation that might be different from those commonly held in Christendom. We did not intend to be contentious in this discourse neither did we intend to make a case out of it. It is just that, as was earlier mentioned, these facts were presented to me in a scripturally consistent and irresistible manner, and at the end I was impressed upon to share it with believers so that we can all wash one another's feet and fight a successful fight of faith. As for whether these views are correct, one thing is certain; wisdom is justified by her children and the Holy Scripture remains the standard.

We have in this book extensively examined the nature and intricate strategies of our enemy in this great resistance. **We arrived at the humble submission that this great resistance against God's place in the lives of the saints and against all godliness is what is referred to in the scriptures as the Great Tribulation.** We also realized that the seven–headed beast has been the major vessel in the hand of the dragon for exercising this great resistance against all godliness. We also saw that the seventh head of the beast represents the Roman Empire. Historical records show that the Roman Empire systematically metamorphosed into the present Western World, which is currently bearing rule over the governments of the world. The records of scripture, concerning this last beast is that as the kingdom is seen to be partly made up of clay and iron; that the kingdom shall be divided. It shall be partly strong and partly broken. Thus, this last beast first operated as an autocratic Empire which is iron (strong) and later as a subtle western world under the cover of western civilization (mixture of clay and iron) which seem to be divided and weak, yet with the strength of iron bearing rule over the entire world.

In the records of history (*American Encyclopaedia, Vol.23, P.729*) "the people of the old Roman Empire cared for nothing else but bread and circuses (i.e food and pleasure/entertainment). It was a materialistic, acquisitive and status conscious society." These things that made up the socio-political and cultural legacies of the old Roman Empire were the same things that metamorphosed into the present sophisticated western civilization. The western world is bearing rule over the world by virtue of the western civilization and will continue till the coming of Christ. This civilization which in our studies comes under the world systems has been neatly packaged and distributed over all the nations of the world. It was designed and introduced by the whore via the beast. Scriptural records show that this last beast is much more sophisticated, dreadful and diverse from those that operated before it. To this end it will accomplish much more at wrecking and devastating the rest of all the inhabitants of the earth. The diabolical effects of these world systems on the churches (saints) have been the gradual but effective erosion of every form of godliness as the case is today.

We also discovered that this beast will trample the residue (i.e. the rest of all mankind including the saints) under feet and that after he would have succeeded in scattering the power of the holy people, then shall the end come. This is what is exactly happening today! Therefore brethren we face an imminent danger of death if nothing is done about our carelessness or lack of knowledge in this warfare with the whore and her cohorts. It is painful to note that for lack of this

8.0 Conclusion

knowledge, a host of us are compromising and perishing consistent with Paul's view that ignorance of our enemy's strategies makes us vulnerable[1]. However, they that do know their God shall be strong and do exploit[2]. They shall turn many unto righteousness and shall take the kingdom of heaven by force[3]. But it seems many of us have forgotten that a warrior should not entangle himself with the affairs of this life. *As I behold this scourge of worldliness ravage and overtake the roots of godliness in the church, I mourn!* We have been so ripped off by our enemy.

Be it known to us brethren that we shall all be individually held accountable if we allow ourselves to be deceived with various doctrines of demons that loom over the churches today. Jesus categorically forewarned us that troops of deceivers shall come in sheep's and shepherd's clothing; and they will lead many astray and if possible the very elect[4]. Paul categorically reminded us that these servants of the dragon have transformed and disguised themselves into ministers of righteousness[5]. We should therefore be at full alert.

From our studies we also traced the cause of this widespread abomination of worldliness among the saints to the unearthed root of **self** in us. We took note of the fact that there is a natural alliance/accord between the **'self'** in man and the **'world'**, bringing us to the conclusion that there is any enemy within and an enemy outside. We determined therefore that our battle plans must be drawn and waged on these two fronts if we are to overcome.

The house of the Lord is devastated, ravaged and almost swallowed up by the whore, and most of our Father's house has now been turned into citadels of merchandize. The Lord is now asking; who shall stand in the gap to cry "vengeance", to reward unto the whore double as she caused us? Therefore came forth the question: when the King of kings shall come shall He find on the earth those that will not rest day and night crying out for vengeance against the whore[6]. In Amos 6:1-6 the Lord said "Woe unto them that are at ease in Zion; who do not show any concern or grief over the desolation of Zion, who are satisfied in their accomplishments and feel secure in the enclave of their successes and affluence, whereas the house of the Lord lieth desolate."

We have laboured by the grace of God to expatiate on all the resistance we may face as mentioned by Christ, in our bid to make it to our eternal habitation. The onus to OVERCOME therefore rests on our shoulders. Christ has made all necessary provisions for us to triumph and to come out of the Great Tribulation without spot, wrinkle, blemish or any mark of the beast. The trumpet shall soon sound at a time we least expect it, therefore put on your wedding garments and refill the oil in your lampstands.

Thus the Lamb of God says:

> *And, behold, I come quickly; and my reward is with me, to give to every man according as his work shall be*[7].

END NOTES

1. 2Cor.2:11
2. Dan.11.32
3. Matt.11:12
4. Matt.24:5,11,24
5. 2 Cor.11:14-15
6. Lk.18:7-8
7. Rev.22:12

www.ingramcontent.com/pod-product-compliance
Ingram Content Group UK Ltd.
Pitfield, Milton Keynes, MK11 3LW, UK
UKHW022212230426
12048UKWH00016BA/806